PROTECTING THE VULNERABLE

SOCIAL ETHICS AND POLICY SERIES
Edited by Anthony Dyson and John Harris
Centre for Social Ethics and Policy, University of Manchester

EXPERIMENTS ON EMBRYOS
Anthony Dyson and John Harris (eds)

THE LIMITS OF MEDICAL PATERNALISM
Heta Häyry

PROTECTING THE VULNERABLE

Autonomy and consent in health care

*Edited by Margaret Brazier and
Mary Lobjoit*

London and New York

First published 1991
by Routledge
11 New Fetter Lane, London EC4P 4EE

Simultaneously published in the USA and Canada
by Routledge
a division of Routledge, Chapman and Hall, Inc.
29 West 35th Street, New York, NY 10001

Typeset in 10/12 pt Garamond by Selectmove
Printed and bound in Great Britain by T J Press (Padstow) Ltd, Padstow,
Cornwall

British Library Cataloguing in Publication Data
Protecting the vulnerable: autonomy and consent in health care.
1. Health services. Ethics
I. Brazier, Margaret II. Lobjoit, Mary
174.2

Lbirary of Congress Cataloging in Publication Data
Protecting the vulnerable: autonomy and consent in health care/
edited by Margaret Brazier and Mary Lobjoit.
p.   cm. – (Social ethics and policy)
Includes bibliographical references and index.
1. Medical ethics.   2. Informed consent (Medical law)
3. Physician and patient.   I. Brazier, Margaret.   II. Lobjoit,
Mary.   III. Series.
[DNLM: 1. Ethics, Medical.   2. Informed Consent.   3. Patient
Participation.   W 50 P967]
R724.P76   1991
174'.2–dc20
DNLM/DLC
for Library of Congress 91–18609

ISBN 0–415–04697–1

CONTENTS

NOTES ON
CONTRIBUTORS

Margaret Brazier is Professor of Law, and Legal Studies Director of the Centre for Social Ethics and Policy, University of Manchester. She is author of *Medicine, Patients and the Law* (1987) and editor of *Street on Torts* and *Clerk and Lindsell on Torts*. She has published widely on medico-legal issues in legal and medical journals.

Alastair Campbell, after being Senior Lecturer in the Department of Christian Ethics and Practical Theology in the University of Edinburgh, is now Professor of Biomedical Ethics in the University of Otago, New Zealand. He is the author of several works on medical ethics including *Moderated Love* (1984).

Heather Draper has a Ph.D. in Medical Ethics and is a Lecturer in Social Ethics at St Martin's College, Lancaster. She has published on ethics and women's issues.

Gavin Fairbairn worked as a psychiatric social worker and in special education before becoming Senior Lecturer in Education, North East Wales Institute of Higher Education at Wrexham. He has co-edited *Psychology, Ethics and Change* (1987) and *Ethical Issues in Caring* (1988).

Raanan Gillon is doubly qualified in medicine and philosophy. He is editor of the *Journal of Medical Ethics* as well as being Director of the Imperial College Health Service and serving as Visiting Professor of Medical Ethics, St Mary's Hospital School/Imperial College and King's College, University of London.

Harry Lesser is Senior Lecturer in Philosophy at the University of Manchester. He is the co-author of *Political Philosophy and Social Welfare* (1980) and co-editor of *Ethics, Technology and Medicine* (1988).

Richard Lindley is a philosopher who until recently lectured at the University of Bradford. He has now completed the academic stage of legal training and is working as a Trainee Solicitor. His publications include *Autonomy* (1986) and *The Values of Psychotherapy* (1989).

Mary Lobjoit is Administrative Director of the Centre for Social Ethics and Policy and was, until 1989, Deputy Director of the Student Health Service, University of Manchester.

Peter Mittler is Professor of Special Education at the University of Manchester and Director of the Centre for Educational Guidance and Special Needs. He has an international reputation in the field and is an adviser to several United Nations organizations.

Colin Morley is an Honorary Consultant Paediatrician at Addenbrooke's Hospital, Cambridge, and University Lecturer at the Cambridge School of Clinical Medicine. His work with babies born at 23–29 weeks' gestation is internationally renowned.

Richard Nicholson worked for some years as a paediatrician and headed the Institute of Medical Ethics' working party, which produced its report on *Medical Research with Children: Ethics, Law and Practice* in 1986. Recently he founded and edits the *Bulletin of Medical Ethics*.

PREFACE

In 1988 the Centre for Social Ethics and Policy, University of Manchester, sponsored its second annual public lecture series, on the theme 'Autonomy and Consent: Protecting the Vulnerable'. Whether in relation to patients, potential research subjects or those vulnerable by virtue of their age, nature or position in society there are numerous problems which were addressed in their specialized ways by our lecturers. These included Dr Colin Morley, Dr Richard Nicholson, Professor Peter Mittler, Professor Margaret Brazier and Dr Raanan Gillon. Our other invited contributors have added their explorations of the achievement of personal freedom in its many guises to the medical, legal, ethical, theological, historical and policy dimensions of autonomy and consent.

M.B. and M.L.
Centre for Social Ethics and Policy
University of Manchester, 1990

ACKNOWLEDGEMENTS

The wide variety of situations within which problems of autonomy and consent arise means that we, the editors, have cause to be grateful to many of our colleagues for their help and advice in preparing this second volume of essays for the Centre for Social Ethics and Policy in Manchester. We thank Deborah Robey, who skilfully typed many of the manuscripts. University staff in both administrative and academic spheres have given freely of their time and thought to the project. Harry Lesser of the Department of Philosophy has been particularly generous in this way. We are especially grateful to Diana Kloss, Professor Leslie Turnberg, Professor Graham Bird and Professor Anthony Dyson, who chaired sessions in the lecture series with their usual patience and good humour. John Harris and Anthony Dyson, our fellow directors of the Centre for Social Ethics and Policy have, as always, been a vital source of wise guidance and encouragement.

INTRODUCTION

'Every human being of adult years and sound mind has a right to determine what shall be done with his own body' (JUSTICE CARDOZO: *Schloendorff* v. *Society of New York Hospital* (1914)). Few doctors, lawyers or ethicists would dissent from Justice Cardozo's ringing declaration of the patient's right to autonomy. But implementing the principle in practice has proved more problematic. Consent to medical treatment and/or participation in clinical research demands that the patient is informed of what she is consenting to. How much information must she be given? In England the courts have so far defined adequate information by reference to accepted practice in the medical profession, whereas in Canada and parts of the USA the test is set by what patients would want to know. In the case of babies, children and mentally handicapped people the question is what criteria apply to determine whether the person is competent to give consent and, if she is not competent, who acts on her behalf to protect her interests.

The general ethical and legal problems of consent become even more complex in the context of research. An adult may properly decide to subject herself to personal risk to benefit the community and the advance of medical knowledge. Should parents be able to subject a child to similar risk even in circumstances where no benefit to that child is envisaged? Are parents competent to take such decisions? Where a baby is born at 23–24 weeks should the judgement on her treatment and possible inclusion on clinical trials be for her parents, or for the qualified medical staff caring for her?

In 1988 the Centre for Social Ethics and Policy, University of Manchester, sponsored its second annual public lecture series. The theme was consent in relation to vulnerable members of society. Whether such persons are patients, potential research subjects or

1

vulnerable individuals by virtue of their youth, or nature, or position in society, they have, and they pose, numerous problems in society. The first five chapters in this volume are based on the lectures given in the Spring of 1988 by Colin Morley, Richard Nicholson, Peter Mittler, Margaret Brazier and Raanan Gillon. Further dimensions to the debate on autonomy are provided by invited contributors who address theological, philosophical, medical and policy dimensions of the struggle to achieve autonomy. These contributions are developed by Heather Draper, Alastair Campbell, Gavin Fairbairn, Harry Lesser, Richard Lindley and Mary Lobjoit from papers first delivered at a March 1988 seminar on Autonomy and Consent jointly organized by the Centre and the Department of Philosophy at Manchester University.

Colin Morley is a distinguished paediatrician. He writes on the practical problems and ethical dilemmas encountered in the care of the newborn infant. A baby is born prematurely. She is tiny and fragile and without immediate medical intervention she will die. Her parents will be distraught. Perhaps the mother will still be semi-conscious if the baby has been delivered by Caesarean section under a general anaesthetic. The parents need care as much as the baby. Can they at that time give any meaningful consent on their child's behalf? Where in the care of the newborn does the line lie between treatment and research? If a baby will die without some novel treatment, is that research or treatment? Finally Dr Morley pleads the case for facilitating proper research on the newborn for the benefit of children yet unborn.

Richard Nicholson practised as a paediatrician for many years. Now he concentrates on writing on ethics. He reviews the dispute about the morality of research on children. It has been argued that non-therapeutic research on any child is always unethical. Parents are not entitled to subject their child to a procedure from which the child herself will obtain no benefit. Dr Nicholson refutes that absolutist stance. He points out that parents do expose their children to non-beneficial risks every day. Driving to the tennis club so mum can play tennis exposes the child in the back to a risk he never consented to. Hence Dr Nicholson argues that if the potential benefit to all children of a research project is great, an individual child may be subjected to some low degree of risk. He highlights too the importance of involving the child herself as soon as she is old enough to have some understanding of what is proposed.

Peter Mittler and Margaret Brazier look at another group of

vulnerable patients: people with mental handicap. Professor Mittler writes from the perspective of the professional involved in the care of those with mental handicap. He asks how far the patients are the victims of the good intentions of the professionals. How may the interests of people with mental handicap best be defined and how can they be best involved in their own care and take control of their own lives? He touches on the controversy over community care. Professionals believe that it is the best option for many people with mental handicap, but do the patients? Margaret Brazier addresses legal questions relating to patients with mental handicap. How does the law define competence to consent to treatment? If a patient is competent, can a refusal of treatment be overruled as 'irrational'? She looks at the absence in England of any provision for proxy consent for adults. And she considers whether some form of adult guardianship really would be effective to safeguard the interests of vulnerable patients.

Raanan Gillon takes an overview of the ethical dilemmas in clinical research and consent to treatment. He subjects the arguments on the legality or otherwise of research on children, and other vulnerable patients, to rigorous philosophical analysis. How can the concept of autonomy be applied to a child? What powers may properly be accorded to a parent? How far may utilitarianism be invoked to justify subjecting A to a risk to benefit C, D and E? Like Richard Nicholson and Colin Morley, Raanan Gillon argues eloquently the need for research and the importance of such research being effectively scrutinized by the community as a whole.

Heather Draper's chapter focuses on a rather different topic: she examines attitudes to female sterilization. She contends that women are abused both by being subjected to sterilization to which they have not given a 'real' consent, and by being refused sterilization when they request it. Heather Draper attacks entrenched attitudes to women's fertility in the health care professions. She develops the themes of autonomy and consent within the context of one highly controversial form of treatment.

Alastair Campbell and Gavin Fairbairn both consider the needs as well as the rights of vulnerable patients. Alastair Campbell argues cogently that dependency is not the enemy of autonomy. For an individual ever to attain autonomy, dependency may be a vital stage in his progress to full autonomy. Children need to be educated into autonomy. Every adult at stages in her life will need and desire to be dependent on others. Autonomy embraces the choice to be dependent when dependency is essential to full health and well-being. Gavin Fairbairn addresses the vexed problem of suicide and paternalism. Many attempted suicides are not considered attempts at self-destruction but 'gestured' suicides, cries for help. So how may the health professionals properly respond? Leaving the unconscious patient to die may be acting to protect her autonomy, or denying her demand for help, her attempt to be dependent. The doctor is truly in a dilemma. And what of the rights of others? Gavin Fairbairn argues that the psychological trauma to family, friends and professionals dealing with a suicide demands that their interests be given proper consideration in the ethical debate.

Richard Lindley and Harry Lesser take the debate a stage further. What information is a patient entitled to in order to give a meaningful consent to treatment? The Canadian Supreme Court has asserted that patients have a right to be told whatever the prudent patient would want to know. English judges disagree. Richard Lindley confronts the ghost that haunts the debate on informed consent in England; the ghost bears to lawyers the name of *Bolam*. For the layperson the judgment in *Bolam* may best be encapsulated in the phrase 'doctor knows best'! Dr Lindley mounts a ferocious attack on the ghost of *Bolam* and its implications for health care. Harry Lesser offers a philosophical analysis of the right to information. He examines the 'medical model' within which the doctor, the professional, judges what information her patient needs, and compares that older model with the alternative model within which patients judge what patients need. Like Lindley, Harry Lesser firmly endorses patients' rights to full information about treatment. Otherwise consent becomes a myth and patient care suffers.

Finally Mary Lobjoit completes this series of essays with an examination of the practical problems faced by doctors dealing with 'borderline' patients. Drawing on her experience as a student health physician, she illustrates the difficulties in caring for patients growing into autonomy. When patients swerve from autonomy to dependence and back again in the course of a consultation, how should the professional respond?

1

WITHOUT THEIR CONSENT?

Working with very premature babies

Colin Morley

It is obvious that the babies who are the focus of this chapter are not able to give their own consent and so primarily it is their parents from whom we are seeking consent for treatment of any kind, or for allowing their child to be part of a research study. Professor P. Tizard, of Oxford, has always put up a very strong argument that the premature babies now surviving and suffering less handicap do so as a result of what has been learnt by doctors from previous generations of babies.[1] Therefore today's babies would, if they could do so, feel it a duty to give their consent (as a way of giving thanks) to allow doctors to learn new things from them which will, in turn, benefit future babies.

There are many difficult problems in working with very premature babies and their parents. The majority of these problems are, of course, related to the practical problems of their management and medical treatment. However, it is inevitable that the issue of research and the obtaining of informed consent for such studies becomes even more important in neonatal intensive care situations.

I shall, first of all, outline the main problems presented by these premature babies and the complexities of their care so that the ethical problems may be considered against this background. About 2 per cent of babies are born two months early, that is at less than thirty-two weeks' gestation. They have a high incidence of disease and physiological problems and almost all need intensive medical and nursing care. In the early 1970s most of these babies, if born at this early gestational age, died. However, the care of these babies has advanced rapidly during the 1980s so that the majority now survive and develop and grow up to be normal children.

5

Unfortunately, in their early days many premature babies are seriously ill and develop a number of major problems. At birth they easily become asphyxiated and require skilled resuscitation. Many of them may then progress to respiratory failure and the need for support with oxygen and artificial ventilation. During this treatment they can develop a rupture of the lung (pneumothorax) and progress to chronic lung disease. They are also in danger of bleeding into the cerebral ventricles and surrounding brain tissue. Hypotension and cardiac depression are common soon after birth and heart failure secondary to a patent ductus arteriosus occurs in many. They are usually unable to feed and have to be fed intravenously or by nasogastric drip. Some of them develop inflammation and perforation of the bowel and others are at a very high risk of developing serious infections such as septicaemia, meningitis or pneumonia. Even in the early 1990s, of the babies born at less than thirty weeks' gestation about a quarter of them die and 5–10 per cent of the survivors have serious handicaps.

The underlying cause of many of these problems and the appropriate treatment still need to be elucidated and refined so that all babies can receive the best care and attention to ensure that they survive to be healthy members of society. The care of these babies is always improving but we are still ignorant about the best ways to manage many of these problems. Over the years paediatricians have learnt to manage these conditions by the traditional methods of reading, learning by experience and copying what other people are doing. They commonly introduce new treatments and techniques into routine clinical practice without asking parental consent. Many treatments have been accepted because of common usage and have never been subjected satisfactorily to careful studies. Treatment is given to a baby because of a background belief of the doctor who considers that it is the best available treatment for the condition. When a doctor is treating a baby he does not tell the parents that another doctor or another baby unit might give the baby a different treatment or have a different policy. The doctor gives the best treatment he knows in those particular circumstances.

It is important that we acquire new knowledge and this must be done accurately, carefully and efficiently so that all babies can benefit from the best treatment in the shortest possible time. How can this be done? The answer is by well-conducted studies into all aspects of diagnosis and therapy.

In modern neonatal intensive care units we are very well aware of the anxiety and stress suffered by the parents of a sick premature baby. At least half of the very premature babies in a large neonatal intensive care unit have been transferred from other hospitals, some just after birth and often with the mother remaining behind. For the mother to go into labour three months early is a great shock, which may be compounded by the mother herself being ill or the baby being sent off to another hospital as an emergency, often in the middle of the night. The parents are desperately worried that the baby will die or survive handicapped, often to such an extent that the mothers are frightened to see their babies. These parents need a great deal of reassurance and help in coming to terms with the baby's problems and their own emotional turmoil.

Those of us who care for the babies also have to care for and support the parents during the first worrying hours, days and weeks. Our job is not only to help the babies but also to instil confidence that the baby is being cared for by sympathetic and skilful professionals who know their job. We try to reduce the level of anxiety by helping parents feel that their baby is in 'good hands' and receiving the best treatment.

It is against this background that I would now like to discuss the topic in hand. Do we always need to ask the parents for consent to study their baby? As paediatricians it is our primary duty to do our best for the baby and family and to do so we must take every opportunity to add to our knowledge so that we can improve the standard of care. This can be done only by carefully conducted studies which are so designed and executed that the results are clear and useful. For many studies there are no problems about obtaining informed consent because the parents are in a physical and emotional state to listen to the background rationally, the doctor has time to describe the protocol and allow them to come to their own conclusion. I firmly believe that all aspects of a child's illness and treatment should be discussed with the parents when it is possible and appropriate. However, there are circumstances where a study would improve care but it is not possible or appropriate to obtain parental consent. Such a study would obviously have been approved by the local ethical committee, which would include a layperson to represent non-medical interests. The purpose of ethical committees is to ensure that studies are sensible, well designed, carry minimal risk to the patient and are likely to produce beneficial information. I shall illustrate the types of studies where I believe consent is difficult to obtain by referring to two examples.

For instance a study might be designed to give a new drug or test a new therapeutic technique to be used as soon as a baby is born, where the baby is suffering from a relatively rare problem. For example, the study may be assessing the efficacy of a drug to prevent serious brain damage in birth asphyxia or it may be a new technique to remove the meconium from the lungs in the case of meconium aspiration. In this type of situation the condition could not be anticipated and even if it could the time would be so short and the parents in such an emotional and physical state that it would not be possible or appropriate to ask for consent. Additionally the condition would be so rare that it would not be reasonable to worry all mothers by asking for consent before labour. If consent was compulsory the study could not be done, the true answer never known and the new treatment would either come into force without proper assessment or never be used. Which would be best for the babies and which is the most ethical standpoint?

A further study might be designed to give a new treatment or to test a new therapeutic technique a few hours after birth, on babies suffering from respiratory distress. For example, the study may be to assess the efficacy of ventilating babies at a rate of eighty breaths per minute compared with forty breaths per minute. At this time the parents are still somewhat shocked by the premature birth, anxious about the baby's future and the future for themselves and their family. They may well be bemused by the equipment surrounding their baby and have not had enough time to understand the treatments she is receiving. The job of the staff at that particular time is to inform them about their baby and her problems, to reassure them that she is receiving the best possible care and attention and to provide emotional and physical comfort. It can be hard at these times then to try to explain dispassionately to such parents that we do not actually know the best way to treat their baby or evaluate the pros and cons of different treatments. It would also be difficult, in these cases, to explain the scientific importance of a randomized trial. I believe that it may not be right to add to their anxiety by asking for consent in some of these circumstances. It can have two effects. First, I have known it considerably undermine parents' confidence that their baby is receiving the best treatment because they come to the conclusion that we do not know what we are doing. Second, the parents may subconsciously, or even consciously, agree to a study simply to ingratiate themselves with the staff hoping to ensure that by so doing their baby receives even better care and attention. I believe that consent under these circumstances is not really informed consent.

If I do not need to ask for consent to initiate a treatment such as artificial ventilation, I find it hard to believe that it should always be necessary to obtain consent for a change in that treatment if it is being done with the baby's best interests in view, and there is a strong possibility that the second treatment might be equally effective if not better than the original one.

In conclusion, neonatal care is advancing very quickly. However, despite appearances, the techniques and treatments need to be evaluated by further appropriate studies. I believe that many of these studies are really a form of internal audit. We are continually asking the questions 'Are we doing our best for the babies? What could we do better?' It is obviously ideal to obtain the consent of the parents, where possible, to enter babies into a new study. However, all studies must have ethical committee approval which should certify that the studies are safe and relevant.

Nevertheless there are some circumstances in neonatal care where it is very difficult, and almost unethical, to try to obtain properly informed consent. In these circumstances if the doctors are always constrained to obtain consent this may either prevent a satisfactory study from taking place or bias the study, because not all the babies with a particular problem would be eligible and it may unnecessarily increase the parents' anxiety level.

Which is the most unethical thing to do? To try to answer a relevant problem without consent, to conduct what one considers to be an inadequate study or never conduct the study so that no one knows the right way to cope with that particular problem? With the added possibility that babies will continue to receive suboptimal care?

I put it to you that informed consent is as important in neonatal studies as in any other situation but by the nature of the problems encountered both in terms of the care of the baby and the parents there are circumstances when the most ethical thing to do is to conduct the study without asking for the parents' consent.

NOTE

1 Personal communication.

2

THE ETHICS OF RESEARCH WITH CHILDREN

Richard Nicholson

The Institute of Medical Ethics set up a working party in 1982 to examine the ethics of research with children and a report was published in 1986.[1] First, I shall describe some of the guidelines which existed before we set up the working party, and some of the results of our own survey on how consent to research on children is handled. Then I will consider some of the empirical work on the ages at which children might be considered to be capable of giving a consent, and finally look at the kinds of things that may be consented to, which will lead into a discussion of what risk means.

There have been many cases of research being conducted, whether on adults or children, in unethical ways which have led to concern about how medical research should be controlled. Examples given in the Nuremberg Trials led to the development of the Nuremberg Code. Since then other research has been done which was not, by anybody's standards, ethical research. Beecher[2] in the 1960s in the USA and Pappworth[3] in Britain published papers and a book detailing examples of the kinds of problems that arise when there is no real control over researchers, with gleams in their eyes about a particular subject, to ensure that they conduct themselves ethically.

The earliest guidelines for the conduct of medical research anywhere date from about 1900, in Prussia. The first ones that I know of are those of the German Ministry of the Interior[4] in 1931; thus even before Nazi doctors started conducting their grotesque experiments there were guidelines in existence. These Directives on Scientific Experimentation were not dissimilar to the principal guidelines now contained in the World Medical Association's Declaration of Helsinki.[5] There was a concern that in dealing with infants or children one must be particularly careful; while the guidelines do not define 'experimentation', there is no suggestion that any sort of experimentation should be entirely forbidden.

Coming to the guidelines still current in Britain, one finds a curious mixture. The fairly strict rules of the Medical Research Council (given in 1963 and never revised)[6] suggest that one cannot undertake research on children that is not directly intended to benefit those children. In 1973 the guidelines of the Royal College of Physicians[7] moved a little way towards permissiveness by suggesting that such procedures (non-therapeutic research) could be conducted if those procedures entailed negligible risk or discomfort. But there is no definition of what is meant by negligible.

The British Paediatric Association guidelines (given in 1980)[8] do not consider at length either legal or ethical problems in the conduct of therapeutic research. What they suggest should be considered in *non-therapeutic research* on children is an examination of the degree of benefit which might result. One example given was that if one was performing a laparotomy on a child for some different purpose, it would be reasonable, while you were inside that child's belly, to do an open biopsy of the kidney if you felt that by getting a normal chunk of kidney you might be contributing greatly to the understanding, for instance, of transplant immunology. One might be able to provide some evidence of why transplanted kidneys are or are not rejected, suggesting that one might obtain great benefit from doing a procedure of no possible benefit to the individual child, who was in any case undergoing a laparotomy for something else. They felt that this was permissible. Now I think that goes further than many people would feel happy with. It was at this point that the Institute of Medical Ethics decided that here was a field in which there was considerable confusion as to what could or could not be permitted; therefore a working party was set up to examine the problem.

Other examples, of the same order as that of the renal biopsy have been published in the British literature in the last few years. For example a paper in *Gut* described work done in India.[9] A group of researchers investigating Indian childhood cirrhosis of the liver wondered whether there was any familial tendency towards this disorder. They performed thirty percutaneous liver biopsies on completely asymptomatic children who had normal liver function to see whether they could find anything in the liver samples which would connect these children with their siblings, who had already developed Indian childhood cirrhosis. In none of the biopsy specimens did they find any abnormality. One wonders why, even if they thought it was permissible to do it, they went on for thirty children? If they had just done ten children, and found nothing, then statistically the likelihood of finding any significant abnormality in other children would be very small. This sort of research may not be done in Britain but has been done elsewhere and is published in British journals.

In our study[1] of the ethics of research on children we did a survey of research ethics committees in England and Wales to see how these bodies, which are supposed to ensure that no unethical research ever takes place, examined the problem of consent in children. We asked, 'Does your committee insist that researchers gain consent from parents or guardians of a child before that child may be entered into a research project?' It is interesting that by no means all the committees who answered that question said that they always did insist on consent: 20 out of 114 committees did not always insist on consent. But at least these results are approaching what most people would feel is the correct position, that one should always require consent for research.

Not all the committees required that parents be given a full explanation of the proposed research; but without a full explanation how does one obtain valid consent? [This question is discussed further in Raanan Gillon's ethical overview of research on the vulnerable in Chapter 5 of this volume.]

Another question asked in the survey, whether consent should be in writing, was answered very variably by the research ethics committees. Few of them required consent to be witnessed by a third party and very few of them required that a parent or guardian be given a copy in writing of either the explanation of the research or the consent form. Similar variations were found when we asked at what age did research ethics committees require that either the consent of an individual child be obtained or his assent (which may not be legally binding consent but an agreement by the child) that he was happy to take part in the research? The ages at which *assent* was required varied from about 10 to 16 years. The ages at which *consent* was required varied from 14 to 18 years. So within Britain there are considerable variations in the way that different committees approach the area of consent.

Let us ask '*What do we mean by consent?*' Perhaps one of the simplest descriptions of its basis is that given by a New York judge, Benjamin Cardozo, just before the beginning of the First World War:[10] 'Every human being of adult years and sound mind has a right to determine what shall be done with his own body.' It is an axiom that has its definitive roots within most systems of philosophy, and also indicates the respect for individuals that one wishes to be part of normal behaviour in society.

Now the problem is that the judge referred to people of adult years being able to give consent. British law allows children to consent to different things at various ages:

- at 5 children may drink alcohol in the home
- at 10 children are considered capable of committing a crime
- at 17 young people may drive a car on the public roads.

In England and Wales 16 was the age at which both girls and boys were considered capable of giving consent to medical treatment. However, this has been modified by the outcome of the *Gillick* case[11] so that the doctor would now assess whether patients younger than 16 are capable of giving consent. While there would be an assumption that at the age of 16 (under the Family Law Reform Act 1969) young people are capable of giving consent, this may be possible at earlier ages provided the child was regarded as capable by his or her doctor. But children have to wait until they are 18 to give blood!

So there is a whole variety of ages at which children are considered capable of various acts, and the law does not help us very much. The final decision in the *Gillick* case has put the onus back on to doctors to decide whether the patient is competent. In deciding whether somebody is capable of giving informed consent, the basic requirements are information, voluntariness and competence. These are generally accepted requirements that, I think, obtain both in Britain and in North America. Most people would say that if you are going to consider a consent given by a patient or research subject to be informed then that person has to be given *information*, but the question of how much information that person has to be given is a matter of considerable argument in different legal systems.

In Britain the case of *Sidaway*[12] allows the amount of information to be that which a responsible body of medical opinion would feel was the appropriate amount to be given, rather than the requirement in the USA that the information to be given is that which a responsible patient would want to know. It tends to be assumed that a responsible patient would actually like to know more than a doctor may wish to disclose.

There needs to be *voluntariness* in consent: there must be no coercion. Coercion may apply in a variety of different ways. It is not unknown for a considerable amount of money to be made available: medical students are most likely to be the recipients of some hundreds of pounds. There was a private research organization in Central London a few years ago that was offering students up to £500 a time to take part in trials of new drugs; some of these trials were fairly risky. I think that would really constitute coercion and would remove the element of voluntariness. One would have to ask very carefully whether the consent those medical students gave was either informed or voluntary.

Then there is the question of *competence* – whether somebody is intellectually able to make a sensible choice. There needs to be evidence of a choice having been made and also that the outcome which is chosen is one that would be regarded by sensible people as being a reasonable outcome. There needs to be evidence of the ability to think rationally and also of comprehension of the information that should have been given.

If one looks at the ability of children to fulfil those requirements there is only a small amount of empirical work; the most relevant is by Weithorn[13] in New York. She took several groups of children and young people, aged from 9 to 21, and posed hypothetical cases to do with depression in children, diabetes, enuresis and epilepsy. During interviews with them they were allowed to ask whatever questions they wanted to obtain the necessary information. Then they were asked for their hypothetical consent to the hypothetical cases. Weithorn found that in most of the different categories of legal requirements children from the age of 14 upwards were behaving just as competently as the 18 and 21-year-old college students that she examined. Even at the age of 9, many children came to make what was seen to be entirely the appropriate decision, but they were unable to give suitable reasons for why they had done so and they did not always show evidence of having comprehended what it was all about. But by the age of 14 the children were doing, on average, as well as the young adults.

A few years earlier Schwartz,[14] a psychiatrist at Yale, studied various children's concepts of research hospitalization. Weithorn's group were normal children in school or college: they were not children who were ill. Schwartz, on the other hand, used a group of children who already had a serious problem in that they were of very short stature. His research was done when growth hormone was just becoming available and they were to be entered into a research programme to see whether growth hormone would help them to gain height. Much time was spent by the psychiatrist and his colleagues on discussion with the children both before and during their admissions for research purposes. The interviews were to explain what the research was all about. Yet when they went back towards the end of the admission and asked the children again none of the children under the age of 11 had any understanding that their admission was concerned with the research project or that they had actually been involved in the research. Also only one-third of the children over the age of 11 had any real understanding of what research was about and what had been going on with them in that hospital. Five of those six children showed very considerable signs of anxiety. Where children are already ill with a chronic disorder, that may greatly influence the outcome of the attempt to inform them.

At the other end of the scale some normal children at a school in Los Angeles in 1975 were asked[15] whether they would take part in a research project involving immunization against swine flu. There was a scare in the USA in 1975 because three recruits at an army base in New Jersey were found to have swine flu; it was feared that it would spread right across the whole country. Scientists quickly developed a vaccine against it and they wanted to try out the vaccine on various groups of people, including children.

In this case the researchers went into classrooms and conducted question-and-answer sessions with the children. All the 7, 8 and 9-year-old groups of children were well able to obtain, as a group, all the necessary information to give an informed consent if they wished to accept being vaccinated. It was only the 6-year-olds who, even as a group, were incapable of asking for all the information that was regarded as necessary by the investigators.

The last bit of evidence about the ages at which people understand things concerns what are called in the United States the Miranda rights. There was a particular case of *Miranda* v. *The State of Arizona*[16] which determined that everybody picked up by the police had both a right to remain silent and a right to legal advice. Research[17] on the ages at which people can understand those rights and act upon them has found that very few children under the age of 14 had any understanding of them but that 15 and 16-year-olds, on the whole, understood as much as adults did. However, 25 per cent of adults who were asked what these basic rights meant failed to give any indication that they understood them. We need to remember when discussing consent that there may be a substantial proportion of our patients or research subjects who, however well we try to inform them, will not be capable of understanding what we are talking about.

Faced with all these very different ages at which children are capable of doing things the working party of the Institute of Medical Ethics came up with some *recommendations*. We suggested that for consent to be valid the consent of the parent or guardian be required at all ages of the child and that the child's assent should be sought from the age of 7 upwards (again by assent we meant not a legally binding consent but that the agreement of the child should be sought).

On a cautious view of the law, we suggested consent be deemed not to have been given if the parent or guardian of a child below the age of 16 refuses consent or if a child over the age of 14 refuses consent. The greater caution comes into the latter case and it needs to be made clear that we did not mean a precise chronological age, but rather the developmental age of an average 14-year-old. Obviously some children are never going to be intelligent enough to understand even by the time of adulthood, but other children may be so bright that they can be fully aware of what we are talking about at the age of 10 years.

The working party discussed consent for *therapeutic research* and suggested that between the ages of 7 and 14 the parent or guardian's decision could override any refusal of assent by a child: it was more likely that a parent or guardian could recognize what was in the interests of the child. But we suggested that if the research was not intended to benefit the child, if it was a *non-therapeutic research procedure*, then it should not be carried out if children aged from 7 years upwards refused assent to it.

Now the question is what are we talking about in terms of what may be consented to. In terms of therapeutic research, where the doctor or researcher intends to benefit the subject of the research, one is on easier ground. But we saw from the earlier guidelines that there is some confusion about non-therapeutic research where there is *no* intention to benefit the child subject, and the intention is merely to perform research. The guideline suggestions that the Institute's working party made were that *proxy consent*, that is consent given by a parent or guardian, to a non-therapeutic procedure *would be legally valid and ethically acceptable only when the risk of such research to the child subject is no more than minimal*. Now one starts getting into difficulties in defining what is meant by minimal risk. The working party came to that conclusion from the legal point of view because it looked at the different attitudes that one might have legally towards parents' duties to their children. It could be said that parents should allow only those actions to be performed on their children which are in their best interests. One could say that the actions have to be in the interests of their child or, and this was the view that prevailed, that actions should merely *not be against* the interests of the child. If one accepts that parents or researchers should not act against the interests of the child then it is reasonable to suggest that non-therapeutic research, provided it is of no greater risk to the child than the sorts of risks it runs in everyday life, would not be against the interests of the child and therefore would be acceptable.

That was the view taken of the current state of the law in Britain. However, there has been a case in Canada[18] which is alarming researchers there because it may outlaw non-therapeutic research on children in Canada. In this case of the sterilization of a mentally retarded woman, the decision went the opposite way to the decisions made in Britain in 1987[19] and 1989[20] when the sterilization of mentally retarded women was permitted by the courts. In Canada, it was decided that the standard that needed to be applied was that doctors must act in the best interests of their patients. To perform an operation on a woman which was not strictly medically indicated by her current medical condition (in other words to sterilize her as a precaution against pregnancy) was not in her best interests and therefore could not be permitted. Whether that case is ever likely to be followed in Britain is doubtful but it is interesting that in Canada now it seems to rule out the possibility of any non-therapeutic research on those not legally competent.

I want to move on to what we mean by *risk*. The working party suggested that, provided that the procedure is of a very low level of risk, it is reasonable for it to be undertaken if it is not intended to benefit the child. There are a variety of different things that you need to do if you are assessing a risk – you need to *identify* what the risk might be, you need to estimate its numerical *size* and then *evaluate* it. If you look at a particular example, such as liver biopsy (mentioned earlier), there are a variety of possible side-effects that might result from it; it is important for practitioners to keep records of how often these side-effects occur. Although disastrous side-effects rarely occur they do happen; likewise there are other risks, such as emotional distress, which may be very much greater in children than in adults. There are problems of parental guilt and what effect that may have on the future relationship between the child and the parent. Regardless of how necessary the liver biopsy is the parents may feel guilty at having allowed their child to go through such a procedure. Merely being in a hospital is quite a risky business and is more so for a child than an adult.

Having identified a risk one needs to estimate the size of it, and there are two aspects to this. There is the probability of an adverse event occurring and there is the magnitude of the harm which arises if the adverse event does occur. When we talk about negligible or minimal risk (the latter term is used in the USA and seems more appropriate) these risks are usually equated with those which are run in everyday life. But there are problems in deciding what are the risks of everyday life. The ratio of the risks involved in the safest job to the most dangerous work is very substantial.[21] Deep sea fishing is 1,000 times more risky than taking part in the manufacture of clothing. Different methods of travel cause considerable variation in the risks to which one is exposed. It is about 1,000 times more likely that one would be killed as a pillion passenger on a motorcycle than if one travels by train, for the same distance travelled. Sporting activities are similarly and variously risky. So one sees the difficulty of trying to work out the risks of everyday life. Should we accept that we expose children, when we are undertaking research on them, to risks as high as those experienced by the passenger on the motorcycle? The levels of risk in medical procedures are sometimes high but the likelihood of death, say during liver biopsy, is much less than that incurred in travelling 1,000 miles by motorcycle. Is it, however, an acceptable risk in a research procedure?

The working party concluded that very small risks have in the past been ignored. For instance smallpox vaccination did go ahead although there was a five per million risk of death from it. Likewise pertussis immunization seems to have been on the borderline of acceptability with a ten per million risk of brain damage. However, in the USA when the risk of major morbidity from swine fever immunization reached ten per million the project was abandoned by the President. Benoxaprofen, a non-steroidal anti-inflammatory drug, was withdrawn when it was shown to have a ten per million risk of death. So one can have some idea of what, in numerical terms, are levels of risk which people tend to ignore within medicine. One has to ask, however, who is doing the ignoring. Is it the doctor or is it the patient? Some work in the United States[22] showed that when you asked paediatricians who were doing research to assess the level of risk of their research procedure you found some fairly curious answers. Some 8 per cent of paediatricians regarded arterial puncture on an infant as being of no or minimal risk. Over half of them regarded a skin biopsy as being of no or minimal risk; yet it is known that a very large proportion of infants on whom one does skin biopsies end up with a scar from it. Three-quarters of the paediatricians regarded admission to hospital of an infant or child under the age of 1 year for 24 hours' observation as being of no or minimal risk. Yet the risk of acquiring any one of a number of different diseases simply by being in a hospital is considerable.

That is what happens when you have doctors assessing risks: you tend to get a slightly rosier view of what the risk levels might actually be than if you ask individual patients or parents.

What I have tried to show is that the whole question of how we decide the level of risk to which you may expose a child is very complicated. In our working party we felt that it was reasonable to expose a child to a very low level of risk when the research was not intended to benefit that child, but that it was not reasonable to act in the way the British Paediatric Association, for instance, has recommended – that provided you as a researcher can convince yourself that there is enough potential benefit, then you can do anything you like. We felt that that was not a suitable approach. We felt that there must be a limit that would be supported by law as well as being one which was ethically correct. We also suggested that the involvement of the child in the process of giving permission for the performance of research is one of a graded involvement. From the age of 7 upwards children should at least be asked for their permission to be involved in research. In some circumstances, even at the age of 7, the child's own feelings about the research should be respected even over the parent's view. By an average developmental stage of 14 years what the child wants is what should be accepted by the researcher.

[Note: Revised versions of the guidelines of the Medical Research Council and of the British Paediatric Association will be published in 1991.]

NOTES

1 R. H. Nicholson (ed.) (1986) *Medical Research with Children: Ethics, Law and Practice*, Oxford: Oxford University Press.
2 H. K. Beecher (1966) 'Ethics and clinical research', *New England Journal of Medicine* 274, 1354–60.
3 M. H. Pappworth (1967) *Human Guinea Pigs*, London: Routledge & Kegan Paul.
4 German Reich (1931) *Circular of the Ministry of the Interior on directives concerning new medical treatments and scientific experiments on man*, translated (1980) in *International Digest of Health Legislation (Geneva)* 31, 408–11.
5 World Medical Association (1964; revised in 1975, 1983 and 1989) *Declaration of Helsinki: Recommendations guiding physicians in bio-medical research involving human subjects*, Ferney-Voltaire, World Medical Association.
6 Medical Research Council (1964) *Responsibility in investigations on human subjects*, in *Report of the Medical Research Council for the year 1962–63*, London: HMSO.
7 Royal College of Physicians (1973, revised 1990) *Supervision of the ethics of clinical research investigations in institutions*, London: Royal College of Physicians.
8 British Paediatric Association (1980) 'Guidelines to aid ethical committees considering research involving children', *Archives of Disease in Childhood* 55, 75–7.
9 N. C. Nayak, N. Marwaha, V. Kalra, S. Roy and O. P. Ghai (1981) 'The liver in siblings of patients with Indian childhood cirrhosis: a light and electron microscopic study', *Gut* 22, 295–300.
10 Cited in R. Faden and T. Beauchamp (1986) *A History and Theory of Informed Consent*, Oxford: Oxford University Press.
11 *Gillick* v. *West Norfolk and Wisbech Area Health Authority* [1984] 1 All E.R. 365; [1985] 1 All E.R. 533; [1985] 3 All E.R. 402.
12 *Sidaway* v. *Board of Governors of the Bethlem Royal Hospital and the Maudsley Hospital* [1984] 1 All E.R. 1018, CA; [1985] 1 All E.R. 643, HL.
13 L. A. Weithorn and S. B. Campbell (1982) 'The competency of children and adolescents to make informed treatment decisions', *Child Development* 53, 1589–98.
14 A. H. Schwartz (1972) 'Children's concepts of research hospitalization', *New England Journal of Medicine* 287, 589–92.
15 C. E. Lewis, M. A. Lewis and M. Ifekwunigue (1978) 'Informed consent by children and participation in an influenza vaccine trial', *American Journal of Public Health* 68, 1079–82.
16 *Miranda* v. *Arizona* [1966] 348US436.

17 T. Grisso (1981) *Juveniles' Waiver of Rights: Legal and Psychological Competence*, New York: Plenum.
18 *Re Eve* (1981) 31 D.L.R. (4th) 1.
19 *Re B (A minor) (wardship sterilisation)* [1987] 2 All E.R. 206, H.L.
20 *F v. West Berkshire Health Authority* [1989] 2 All E.R. 545, H.L.
21 E. E. Pochin (1982) 'Risk and medical ethics', *Journal of Medical Ethics* 8: 180–4.
22 J. Janofsky and B. Starfield (1981) 'Assessment of risk in research on children', *Journal of Pediatrics* 98, 842–6.

3

COMPETENCE AND CONSENT IN PEOPLE WITH MENTAL HANDICAP

Peter Mittler

People with mental handicap are in greater danger of being victims of the good intentions of others than most other marginalized groups. It is precisely because of their intellectual limitations that others make decisions for them. These decisions can be fundamental – beginning with the right to life itself. Later decisions fundamentally affect the quality of life and services, for example, the extent to which people are in the company of non-handicapped persons in school, in the neighbourhood, in where and with whom they live, in their choice of friends and partners, in the expression of their sexuality. At the level of daily living, basic choices are often not available in food, clothes, friends or activities. We tend to assume that people with mental handicap do not have the ability or the experience to make or to express such choices. In any case, it is often more convenient to decide on their behalf.

What, then, is the basis of our beliefs about what is bad and good practice in the field of caring for people with mental handicap? How do we know that our goals and methods are justified? What are our own motives and interests? How can we know whether we are acting in the best interests of mentally handicapped persons? Above all, how can people with mental handicap themselves take part in discussion and decision-making; how can we genuinely consult them? What would constitute informed consent? Do the criteria for consent require redefinition if the person is asked to make choices in situations where the alternatives have not been

22

experienced in reality or in imagination? Does a capacity for choice demand a minimum level of experience or intellectual activity? Can this be acquired through education and training?

In our concern to improve the condition of people with mental handicap, we have not given ourselves enough time to analyse the moral and ethical assumptions behind our efforts. This is all the more important now that there is a growing consensus about the rights of people with mental handicap and about the kinds of services which should be made available. It is generally assumed that our efforts to develop community-based services are morally justified because they offer a better quality of life than segregated or institutional services. Even if we agree that this is the case, we should constantly question the validity of the moral and ethical assumptions which underlie our belief systems and decisions. Once we begin to do this, we shall find many contradictions and inconsistencies between our ideals and the realities of daily life experience of people with mental handicap. The implication here is not that we should return to old practices but that we should be more rigorous in questioning the quality of community provision.

THE PRINCIPLE OF NORMALIZATION (SOCIAL ROLE VALORIZATION)

A major influence on the development of measures of quality assurance has been normalization theory, later renamed social role valorization.[1] The theory is primarily concerned with the extent to which a person with mental handicap plays – and is seen to play – a socially valued role in society.

The principle of normalization has been immensely influential in North America and Europe and has provided the underlying rationale and moral justification for the movement not only to bring people with mental handicap into the mainstream of community life but also to ensure that they are regarded as full citizens with equal rights to community facilities and services. In the UK, the preferred terminology is in terms of the 'ordinary life' model, following a series of clearly written, practical guidance documents which have come from the King's Fund Centre,[2] and the Independent Development Council for People with Mental Handicap.[3]

But we still have to ask 'Whose ordinary life?' Most of us live in a diverse, complex and above all highly pluralist society, with people with vastly differing beliefs and value systems. What are the criteria by which we assess whether a person with mental handicap is living an ordinary life or, indeed, wishes to do so? The theory has also been criticized as largely irrelevant to the conditions of life in developing countries where the concept of a valued life is reserved for a small elite.[4] Even in developed countries, the principle that people with mental handicap should have full access to the same services used by all members of the public is having to confront the reality of the underfunded and sometimes undervalued public services which fail to meet the needs of the population as a whole. This dilemma is acutely reflected in decisions about how the needs of elderly people with mental handicap can be met in societies in which non-handicapped elderly people are often living in conditions of gross poverty and deprivation.[5]

Some of the criticisms arise from a misconception that it is the individual rather than the environment that is to be normalized. Criticisms have also been made about the less than accessible writing style of some of its principal proponents. More fundamentally, Rose-Ackerman, writing from the standpoint of logic and ethics, analysed a number of internal inconsistencies arising from the principle of normalization and concluded that 'this slogan appears to have outlived its usefulness'.[6] Nevertheless, it has survived as probably the most influential body of theory in the field of services for people with mental handicap.

We must guard against romanticizing the advantages of community living. People with mental handicap can be as much at risk of loneliness, oppression and devaluation in modern, enlightened community services as in the bad old institutions. They may live, learn and work in the community but still have little opportunity to express an opinion, to make informed choices between alternatives or to acquire the kind of hard-won autonomy and independence which is enjoyed by others of their age. A child can attend an ordinary school but can still be socially and educationally isolated. An adult living in an ordinary house or apartment may be isolated and lonely, may never speak to neighbours, use local shops or enjoy ordinary recreational activities. People discharged from long-stay hospitals and living in ordinary houses have become the targets of hostility and victimization by neighbours.[7] Flynn (1988)

WHO DETERMINES WHOSE NEEDS?

At the centre of these discussions are the individuals with a mental handicap about whom decisions are being made. Must others always speak on their behalf? In what sense can they be helped to express an opinion and how valid is that opinion? Should we not do more to teach them to make informed decisions for themselves and what form should such assistance take?

In many countries the concept of *need* has come to assume central importance in decision-making. But who determines needs? What part does the individual play in identifying these needs? All too often it is professionals and service providers whose assessment of the individual's needs determines the services provided, sometimes with the advice of family members. The person with mental handicap is hardly ever consulted; by definition, such a person is thought to be incapable of consultation or consent.

Needs arising from impairments are not exclusively intrinsic to the individual. They depend in part on the opportunities for the satisfaction of those needs which can be provided by the environments in which the person is living and learning. A child may require additional educational provision in one school but not in another. One school may have the means to meet the child's needs within its existing resources whereas a second school may not be able to do so without extra provision. In that sense, the concept of need is both relative and interactive.

Needs arise from an interaction between limitations within the person and those that spring from the environment – for example, inappropriate teaching, inaccessible curriculum, unfavorable attitudes, as well as physical barriers requiring ramps and lifts. Identification of needs is then a starting-point for the design of an individual education programme (IEP) which is unique to the individual but which aims to modify the environment as much as to compensate for the person's impairments or difficulties.

Unfortunately, the pervasive terminology of individual need has become synonymous with what can realistically be provided within limited financial and human resources. In the UK, for example, national surveys of the implementation of the Education Act 1981 suggest that official statements on individual children tend to invoke the concept of need to justify recommendations which represent the only possible placement – generally in a special school rather than in an integrated setting.[8] My concern here is not with the arguments for and against integration but with the ethical implications of decision-making on behalf of individuals whom it is not considered possible to consult.

PARTICIPATION IN DECISION-MAKING

There are very few studies in which children or young people themselves have been asked for their views. In the national survey of the practice of some 100 Local Education Authorities in England and Wales, only one reported that pupils were regularly consulted in the process of identifying their needs and making decisions about their schooling.[9] This study was reporting on procedures for assessing children with a very wide range of special educational needs, many of whom would have been quite capable of expressing an opinion on their future schooling.

Encouraging pupil participation in assessment and decision-making is one of the elements of good practice recommended in official guidance issued in the United Kingdom. More special schools seem to be encouraging pupil participation in discussion of their own situation and trying to involve them in a consideration of alternative courses of action. Even where children with severe learning difficulties are concerned, a significant number of pupils can contribute to a discussion and can give an opinion of their own, at least by the time they are ready to leave school. It is not uncommon for pupils to be involved in school-based case conferences and review meetings; indeed many teachers try to prepare their pupils for discussions of this kind. Such preparation may include training on how to take part in meetings, listening to others, taking turns, not interrupting and other elements of 'good committee practice'. In addition, some pupils are given 'assertiveness training', along lines developed for other minority or disadvantaged groups or for individuals who feel in need of such support. Training in social skills, including self-assertiveness, could be critical once pupils leave school and encounter discrimination and negative attitudes on the part of professionals or members of the public.

Preparation of older school age pupils for participation in review meetings and case conferences is also an essential preparation for similar meetings which are likely to become a more frequent feature of adult services. Adults with mental handicap are increasingly participating in 'goal planning' meetings. Several accounts have been published in Britain, including those from the NIMROD project in South Wales,[10] and an excellent working manual from the Open University.[11]

SELF-DETERMINATION AND SELF-ADVOCACY IN ADULTS

Self-determination and self-advocacy are central to the goal of independence of adults with a mental handicap. Although it is a truism to state that the degree to which adults can achieve independence will vary greatly from person to person, it is equally true to say that their abilities are frequently underestimated, even by those who know them well.

One of the most impressive achievements of people with mental handicap is reflected in the growth of self-advocacy groups. Starting in Sweden, North America and later spreading to Australia, New Zealand, Britain and several other countries, people with mental handicap have been setting up and running their own organizations, electing their own officers and holding meetings to discuss their situation. Many have developed mutual support and self-help groups and also addressed meetings of non-handicapped people, including conferences and seminars. The last three world congresses of the International League of Societies for Persons with Mental Handicap (ILSMH) as well as several regional conferences have provided a forum for people with mental handicap not only to meet together but also to run plenary sessions and interact as fellow delegates with other participants. People First organizations have now developed in many countries and in different settings, usually local, sometimes national. One international meeting has also been held and more are planned. Consumer committees have been developed in some facilities such as day or residential centres, generally with unobtrusive participation and support from professional staff.[12]

The growth of the self-advocacy movement calls for a reappraisal of our concept of the status and competence of people with mental handicap. On the one hand, we should warmly welcome such developments, as a natural stage in the evolution of the very independence which we claim always to have been our aim in working with mentally handicapped people. If we are serious in listening to the voice of the consumer, we shall need to find ways of involving them to a much greater extent than in the past in participating in discussions on the services which are provided, as well as in their own programmes of rehabilitation. They may need preparation and support in self-advocacy but experience during the 1980s suggests that this can be given, once parents and professionals are convinced that this is both a necessity and a right.

At the same time, the ability of people with mental handicap to represent their own interests could lead to conflicts with professionals and service planners and providers and also with parents. What happens, for example, if parents insist that their adult son or daughter is 'not ready' to begin a programme of road safety training, to learn to go to a cafeteria or to local shops, to have sex education or to develop a sexual relationship? But if we consult people with mental handicap, are we not committed to respecting and valuing what they have to say?

The movement to run down or close the larger residential institutions provides another example of a possible conflict of interest between professionals and mentally handicapped people whose interests they claim to represent. What if individual residents make it clear that they do not wish to be relocated to an ordinary house in the community? After all, many people have lived in hospitals for so long that it has become their home, the centre of all their friendships and recreational interests. A few have had experience of hostel or group home provision and have chosen to return to hospital.

What are the implications of such a dilemma? Policy-makers and many professionals are convinced that community provision is superior to institutional living because living in the community is thought to be intrinsically better and a more 'valued' way to live. But the individuals to be rehoused are not necessarily persuaded and may protest at the upheaval to which they are being subjected. How far should their wishes be respected? If not, how could this be justified? Would they try to do so by referring to their lack of experience of community facilities? Would the argument be finally settled by the closure of the hospital?

These are complex and sensitive areas about which dogmatic expressions of opinion are inappropriate. But discussion in the public arena does bring out in sharp relief the stereotyped views which many influential people hold about the competence of people with mental handicap, their perceived inability to learn from experience or from instruction. It is also interesting to note the reliance placed by the courts on the concept of mental age, at a time when the use of standardized tests of intelligence is somewhat discredited in professional circles, at least for purposes of prediction and placement. Furthermore, mental handicap is still seen largely as the province of medical specialists. Only rarely is evidence sought from people involved in a caring or teaching relationship with a mentally handicapped person.

QUALITY OF LIFE AND SERVICES

Serious concern with the quality of life of people with mental handicap follows studies which suggest that a number of people discharged from long-stay hospitals were living in substandard accommodation, had little or no work or other activities during the day and were isolated from their neighbours and from community facilities. Some were living in private rented accommodation with very poor facilities.[13]

Attention also needs to be paid to the quality of life of families who are finding it increasingly difficult to continue to look after a seriously handicapped relative without adequate support when they themselves are becoming older and infirm. It is sometimes forgotten that 'care in the community' is not to be equated with permanent care by the family. Indeed, the principle of normalization would indicate that young people with mental handicap should be leaving the family home and living more independently with the degree of personal and social support which they themselves need.

In some cases, families are faced with a choice between low-quality institutional care and continuing to provide a home regardless of the strain which this may impose. In other cases, families are not even aware that viable alternatives are available and that they have the right to initiate discussion of these alternatives. If they do not do so, professionals may prefer to assume that all is well – at least until there is a crisis.

It is against this background that issues of quality assessment and assurance have become much more prominent in recent years. A collection of papers on quality of life issues for people with mental handicap placed strong emphasis on opportunities to make choices between perceived alternatives and to develop autonomy in decision-making.[14] A conference on ethical aspects of intervention and decision-making highlighted a wide range of issues which had

Brown 1988

not previously received detailed attention,[15] including implications for people with profound impairments of intellectual functioning, corresponding in some cases to developmental levels of only weeks or months.[16] ILSMH has also published a booklet reviewing developments in the field of quality assurance and suggesting ways in which family members and consumers themselves could become more involved in monitoring of service quality.[17]

A number of accreditation and evaluation instruments have been explicitly based on principles of normalization (social role valorization). Attempts have been made to assess the value systems underlying service planning and to measure service provision and delivery on a quantitative basis. The best-known instruments are the Program Analysis of Service Systems (PASS),[18] and the later development of PASSING.[19] There are now several other well-tried systems,[20] some of these developed by parent and voluntary agencies themselves, for example the Society for the Intellectually Handicapped in New Zealand and MENCAP in the UK.[21]

CONCLUSIONS: CAN RIGHTS BE TURNED INTO REALITIES?

In the late 1960s ILSMH promulgated the Rights of Persons with Mental Retardation, later adopted almost word for word by the United Nations in its 1971 Declaration. The United Nations later promulgated the Declaration of the Rights of Disabled Persons (1975). ILSMH also developed some concrete guidelines to assist member societies to ask specific questions designed to assess the extent to which these general statements of principle might be reflected in services at grass-roots community level.[22] Since then, various United Nations documents have also tried to provide guidance which goes beyond statements of principle, for example the *World Programme of Action Concerning Disabled Persons* and the *Manual on Equalisation of Opportunities for Disabled Persons*.[23]

But should people with mental handicap have special rights of their own or should they rely on the Universal Declarations of Human Rights? The United Nations has now promulgated a Convention on the Rights of Children; countries adopting this convention would have a quasi-legal obligation to implement its provisions, in contrast to declarations which merely promulgate general principles. The Convention includes sections on the rights of children with disabilities to have full access to health, education, social and vocational training services. The International Labour Organization launched a Convention on Employment of Disabled People (1981); only about twenty countries have so far committed themselves to this Convention. Perhaps a Convention on the Rights of Children will be more successful.

If we consider the quality of life of people with mental handicap on a global scale, we find that the majority of people with mental handicap are relegated to a low status in society. Only rarely do they and their families enjoy a lifestyle that is valued by the rest of society or by responsible public authorities. Despite the many improvements which have taken place in a few countries, there are many others where people with mental handicap are still excluded from their basic rights as human beings. There are frequent reports of children chained to furniture, kept in cages in institutions and deprived of their most basic rights to food, clothing and shelter. There are still countries where children with mental handicap are not given access to any form of education or stimulation, particularly if they are profoundly or multiply disabled or if their behaviour is considered too difficult.

The fate of adults is even worse. Few countries can afford to be satisfied with the quality of services provided for adults with mental handicap. Many adults are totally unprovided for. Some are kept at home without access to training or preparation for community life for as long as their families can keep them. Others become vagrants and beggars, are consigned to the back wards of psychiatric institutions or sent to prison. Even in developed countries, the majority of adults are still congregated together in segregated workshops, even leisure facilities. It is only the lives of a very small minority that reflect our slogans of normalization and community participation or that are consistent with the UN principles of equalization of opportunity. In many countries any discussion of valued lifestyles and full human rights would be an irrelevance, unless there was a real possibility of some action and advocacy which would begin to address their needs.

We live in an age of slogans, principles and ideologies which are often far from the realities of everyday life. For this reason, we must move from principles to practice, monitor the quality of life for people with mental handicap and provide pressure and advocacy to ensure that the slogans of yesterday and today do not remain empty rhetoric.

NOTES

1 W. Wolfensberger (1972) *The Principle of Normalisation in Human Services*, Toronto: National Institute of Mental Retardation (G. Alan Roeher Institute); W. Wolfensberger (1983) 'Social role valorisation: a proposed new term for the principle of normalisation', *Mental Retardation* 21: 234–9.

2 King's Fund Centre (1982) *An Ordinary Life: Comprehensive Locally Based Services for Mentally Handicapped People*, London: King's Fund Centre; (1984) *An Ordinary Working Life: Vocational Services for People with Mental Handicap*, London: King's Fund Centre.

3 D. Towell (ed.) (1988) *An Ordinary Life in Practice*, London: King's Fund Centre.

4 P. Mittler and R. Serpell (1985) 'Services: an international perspective', in A. Clarke, A. D. B. Clarke and J. Berg (eds) *Mental Deficiency: The Changing Outlook* (4th edn), London: Methuen.

5 J. Hogg, S. Moss and D. Cooke (1988) *Ageing and Mental Handicap*, London: Croom Helm.

6 S. Rose-Ackerman (1982) 'Mental retardation and society: the ethics and politics of normalisation', *Ethics* 93: 81–101, p. 97.

7 M. Flynn (1988) *A Home of my Own*, London: Cassell.

8 B. Goacher, J. Evans, J. Welton and K. Wedell (1988) *Policy and Provision for Special Educational Needs*, London: Cassell.

9 ibid.

10 S. Humfreys (1985) *Planning for Progress*, Research Report 18, Cardiff: Mental Handicap in Wales Research Unit.

11 A. Brechin and J. Swain (1987) *Changing Relationships: Shared Action Planning with People with a Mental Handicap*, London: Harper & Row.

12 P. Williams and B. Shoultz (1982) *We Can Speak for Ourselves*, London: Souvenir Press; B. Crawley (1988) *The Growing Voice: A Survey of Self Advocacy Groups in Adult Training Centres in Great Britain*, London: Campaign for People with Mental Handicap.

13 M. Flynn (1988) *A Home of my Own*, London: Cassell.

14 R. Brown (ed.) (1988) *Quality of Life for Handicapped People*, London: Croom Helm.

15 P. Dokecki and R. Zaner (eds) (1986) *Ethics of Dealing with Persons with Severe Handicaps: Towards a Research Agenda*, London and Baltimore, Md: Paul H. Brookes.

16 M. Miles (1986) *Profound Mental Handicap*, Brussels: International League of Societies for Persons with Mental Handicap; C. Whitaker (1989) 'Quality of life and people with a very profound mental handicap', *British Journal of Mental Subnormality* 35: 3–7.

17 International League of Societies for Persons with Mental Handicap (1988) *Quality Evaluation Guidelines: A Means of Renewal and Revitalisation of Services by Voluntary Associations*, Brussels: ILSMH.

18 W. Wolfensberger and L. Glenn (1975) *Program Analysis of Service Systems (PASS)*, Toronto: National Institute of Mental Retardation.

19 W. Wolfensberger and S. Thomas (1983) *PASSING: Program Analysis of Service Systems: Implementation of Normalisation Goals – Normalisation Criteria and Ratings Manual*, Toronto: G. Alan Roeher Institute.

20 J. Beswick, T. Zadik and D. Felce (eds) (1986) *Evaluating Quality of Care*, Kidderminster: British Institute for Mental Handicap.

21 Independent Development Council for People with Mental Handicap (1986) *Pursuing Quality: How Good Are Your Services for People with Mental Handicap?*, London: King's Fund Centre; R. Blunden (1986) 'An overview of five national systems for reviewing quality of services', Brussels: International League of Societies for Persons with Mental Handicap (mimeo); P. Russell (1986) 'Evaluating the quality of services for people with mental handicap: the role of voluntary organisations', Brussels: International League of Societies for Persons with Mental Handicap.

22 International League of Societies for Persons with Mental Handicap (1978) *Step by Step*, in *Choices: Proceedings of 7th World Congress, Vienna*, Brussels: ILSMH.

23 United Nations (1983) *World Programme of Action Concerning Disabled Persons*, Vienna and New York: UN Centre for Social Development and Humanitarian Affairs; United Nations (1986) *Manual on Equalisation of Opportunities for Disabled Persons*, Vienna and New York: UN Centre for Social Development and Humanitarian Affairs.

4

COMPETENCE, CONSENT AND PROXY CONSENTS

Margaret Brazier

'The fundamental principle, plain and incontestable is that every person's body is inviolate.' With these ringing words GOFF L.J. in *Collins* v. *Wilcock* affirmed the individual's autonomy and asserted her right to self-determination over her body.[1] A graphic illustration of the law's role in safeguarding patient autonomy can be found in *Devi* v. *West Midlands A.H.A.*[2] A young Sikh woman who already had three children consented to minor gynaecological surgery. In the course of that surgery the surgeon discovered that her uterus had ruptured. He concluded that any further pregnancy would be hazardous and sterilized her there and then. There is no doubt that the surgeon honestly believed that he had acted in Mrs Devi's 'best interests'. Many women, in Mrs Devi's circumstances, would have agreed with him and thanked him for acting promptly and saving them from the risks of further surgery on some later occasion. But Mrs Devi was distraught. Sterilization contravened her religious convictions. She sued for battery successfully. The surgeon's act constituted a trespass against her person. His evaluation of her 'best interests' and any question of the alleged 'irrationality' of her views were irrelevant. Save in circumstances of dire emergency,[3] a patient's 'best interests' are for the patient to define.

Yet from 1987 to the present day a series of judgments[4] in the English[5] courts have endorsed sterilization of mentally handicapped women and girls in their 'best interests' and without their consent. The House of Lords in *F* v. *West Berkshire Health Authority*[6] have held that a doctor can lawfully operate on, or give other treatment to, adult patients who are incapable, for one reason or another, of consenting to his doing so, provided that the operation or other treatment concerned is in the best interests of the patient.

The 'best interests' of the patient, their Lordships unanimously decided, is to be defined by the *Bolam* test;[7] that is the doctor must, in deciding to operate on or treat the incapable patient, have acted in accordance with a practice accepted at that time as proper by a responsible body of medical opinion skilled in the particular form of treatment in question.[8] In effect her doctor acts as a proxy for the incapable patient. He, on her behalf, authorizes the treatment *he* judges to be in her interests.

Mrs Devi was afforded legal recognition of her right to autonomy albeit the exercise of that right, actual rejection of sterilization, might have imperilled her life, or that of her child in a subsequent pregnancy. Jeanette,[9] *T*[10] and *F*[11] were sterilized on the basis of judgments made by others as to their 'best interests'. The distinction, of course, between Mrs Devi and the other unfortunate young women is that they are judged to be incompetent to define their own interests. The competent patient is legally entitled to evaluate her own interests, however 'irrational' her doctor or society judges that evaluation to be. The incompetent patient enjoys no legal right to autonomy.

That rather facile answer begs several questions which this chapter attempts to examine, if not, alas, to answer. They include

1 What are the criteria by which English law determines in- competence?
2 What are the functions of requirements for consent to treatment and clinical research?
3 In the light of those functions, what provision can be made in the law for safeguarding the interests of vulnerable patients?
4 Would legal recognition of some form of adult guardianship or proxy consents be a desirable reform?

CRITERIA FOR COMPETENCE

No English judgment, to my knowledge, directly addresses the question of how to determine whether or not a patient is incapable of consenting to medical treatment. In the judgments authorizing the sterilization of mentally handicapped women, the patient's incompetence has been assumed. In cases such as *T* v. *T*[12] that assumption is unsurprising. *T*, aged 19, was said to have the mental age of a child of 2, she was largely incapable of speech, was doubly incontinent and had no understanding of the workings of her body. But in other cases the issue of competence is more debatable. Jeanette[13] was 17 and said to have the mental age of 5 to 6 though a more limited ability to communicate. F[14] was a woman of 36 with the mental age of 4 to 5. In one of the most recent judgments[15] authorizing sterilization of a girl under 18, the girl, referred to as P, was again said to have the mental capacity of a 6-year-old, but had relatively good social skills and verbal capacity. These cases seem to me to be nearer the borderline of competence.

An individual's mental capacity has legal relevance in several contexts quite apart from consent to treatment. Does he have the mental capacity to marry, to make a will, to conclude a legally enforceable contract? In English law there is no universal test of mental capacity. The question is decided in the context of the nature of the particular transaction in issue. What might that entail in the context of medical treatment? In *Chatterton* v. *Gerson*[16] BRISTOW J. addressed the problem of what a doctor must tell a patient about proposed treatment in order for her to be able to give a valid consent to that treatment. He held that for consent to be valid the patient must be informed 'in broad terms of the nature and purpose of treatment'. A patient who apparently gave consent, but had been denied such basic information, would have an action against the doctor for trespass to her person. But as long as that basic information was provided by the doctor a failure to disclose information relating to the risks and side-effects of treatment did not vitiate the patient's consent. Any remedy available to the patient lay in negligence for a breach of the doctor's duty of care to provide proper and competent advice as well as treatment.[17]

The test of what a patient must be told to give a valid consent, to authorize treatment, must also be the test of what a patient must understand to be capable of giving a valid consent. Thus for a patient to be competent she need understand only 'in broad terms the nature and purpose of treatment'. She does not need to be able to understand in any sophisticated sense the pros and cons of treatment, nor need she be able to evaluate the risk of a particular treatment nor compare its merits to other available treatments. It seems to follow then that patients cannot be categorized as competent or incompetent, but in respect of any particular procedure the doctor must consider whether the basic nature of that specific treatment is explicable to the individual patient.

Further evidence that competence cannot be determined generally but only in the context of the actual circumstances in which the issue arises can be gleaned from the *Gillick* litigation, and case law on capacity to marry and to make a will. In *Gillick* v. *West Norfolk and Wisbech A.H.A.*,[18] Victoria Gillick asserted that *no* child under 16 could lawfully consent to medical treatment on her own behalf. Four of the five Law Lords categorically rejected that assertion stating that a lawful consent can be given by a child who has reached 'a sufficient understanding and intelligence to be capable of making up his own mind *on the matter requiring decision*'[19] (my italics). Each child patient must be assessed on her own merits. Not every 14-year-old can consent to, say, contraceptive treatment. What is crucial is what that girl understands of what is proposed to her. An individual child of 14 may enjoy the capacity to consent to certain forms of treatment, but not to others whose more complex nature and purpose is beyond her comprehension.[20]

That the test of competence relates to the transaction in issue is further illustrated by the judgment of the Court of Appeal in *In the Estate of Park*.[21] Mr Park had suffered a severe stroke which had impaired his memory and speech. On 30 May 1949 he married his second wife in the morning and in the afternoon he made a complicated will disposing of his considerable property. After his death, the second Mrs Park challenged the will on the grounds that he lacked the sound memory and understanding necessary to make a will. She succeeded on the grounds that on 30 May 1949 Mr Park lacked the necessary mental capacity to make a valid will. Her disgruntled in-laws had, however, challenged the marriage on the grounds that Mr Park was unable to consent to marriage by reason of unsound mind on 30 May 1949. They failed. Mr Park lacked the necessary memory and understanding to dispose of his property but retained sufficient understanding to marry. He understood the nature of the ceremony and the rights and obligations of matrimony.

The extensive case law[22] on testamentary capacity is itself instructive on criteria for competence. Evidence of confusion or dementia in an elderly testator is of itself no ground to invalidate a will.[23] The decline in intelligence must be such as to show that the testator had no meaningful awareness of what he was doing. Loss of speech *per se* does not connote incompetence. A will made by a testator who could communicate only by nods and pressure on the hand was upheld as valid.[24] Nor is competence static. If X was lucid on the day he made the will, it matters not that he was demented the day before and the day after.[25]

This brief survey of other areas of English law serves to reinforce the contention then that the test for competence to consent to medical treatment is simply, can the patient understand what will be done to him and why?

CRITERIA FOR COMPETENCE: LUDICROUSLY BASIC?

Such a standard of competence is obviously pretty minimal. So can it be right? In a number of respects a 'low' competence threshold solves a lot of problems. Prior to the judgment of the House of Lords in *F* v. *West Berkshire Health Authority*[26] health care professionals were on occasion so concerned about the legality of treating mentally handicapped patients that such patients were refused relatively routine treatment, such as dental care, hernia repairs and cataract surgery. Indeed part of the rationale of their Lordships' judgment in *F* that doctors could treat such patients without their consent in their 'best interests' was the laudable desire that patients should not suffer for lack of necessary treatment.[27] But how often are even quite severely mentally handicapped patients incompetent to authorize routine treatment such as dental care or minor surgery?

Consider the example of a patient with a rotten tooth which ought to be extracted. The process for obtaining consent is simple.

1 Does your tooth hurt?
2 Explain how the pain can be stopped.
3 Would you like it taken out?

If the patient assents to (1) and (3) and understands (2) he is competent to authorize that treatment himself.

Sterilization is, of course, treatment of a quite different order, so surely to suggest, as I did earlier, that some of the young women sterilized with judicial blessing might even have been near the borderline of competence must be ludicrous. After all even the least handicapped of those women were said to have mental ages of 5 to 6, and who would say a 5-year-old could consent to sterilization? But what is actually entailed in explaining in broad terms the nature and purpose of sterilization?

1 We would like to do an operation on your tummy.
2 The operation will stop you having babies.
3 Let me explain why it is not a good idea to have babies.

A child of 7 or 8 might well comprehend such information. And Jeanette and the other mentally handicapped women were not in actuality 5 or 6 but 17 and older. They enjoyed in addition to the limited reasoning capacity of the 5 or 6-year-old the experience of puberty and menstruation. Hopefully they had received training and education in the workings of their bodies. The decided cases on treating incompetent patients place great emphasis on mental age yet never attempt to assess what level of comprehension is entailed by such an age.

A minimal level of competence may reduce the numbers of patients unable to authorize treatment for themselves but also generates problems of its own. The most obvious problem is practical. Staff caring for such patients will face difficulties managing patients whose exercise of their right to decide for themselves on treatment must presumably extend to daily care decisions as well. Patient Y refuses to have a bath. He knows that he stinks. He knows the bath will remove the stink but he likes stinking. As he is competent, no one else can define his 'best interests'. Such a state of affairs is ghastly for staff and fellow patients. Perhaps legal criteria for overruling Y's refusal to bath should be contemplated. But we should not pretend that we are acting in Y's interests because he is incapable of deciding the matter for himself.

More disturbing perhaps than the nuisance generated by patient Y, is the dilemma posed by patients who are perceived by their carers as 'irrationally' refusing treatment that undoubtedly would promote their individual welfare. An elderly demented patient retains sufficient understanding and reasoning capacity to comprehend a proposal put to her to remove a diseased tooth. Thus on the minimal test suggested above she remains competent to consent to or refuse such treatment, but nevertheless she allows her fear of dentists and pain to overcome her desire to have the tooth extracted. A mentally disordered patient with a high degree of intelligence completely understands what is entailed in operating on his hernia. He refuses treatment because of his obsessive belief that the surgeon will deliberately kill him to harvest his organs for transplantation.

At first sight it might seem that such 'irrational' treatment refusals should be overridden. Should a child reject similar treatment on the basis of childish fears and misconceptions, her parents may lawfully require her to submit to that treatment. Too swift an acceptance of any proposition that 'irrational' treatment refusals should be invalid should be avoided. How is 'irrationality' to be evaluated? Thousands of patients whose competence is never questioned stay away from dentists out of 'irrational' fear to the detriment of their dental, and sometimes their general, health. Yet it is only patients labelled mentally handicapped or demented who will find their 'irrational' treatment refusals overriden. Pregnancy for thousands of women is a disaster. They are not able, because of poverty, or limited intelligence, or extreme youth, or all these factors, to function as a mother so as to benefit themselves or their children. Only girls labelled as mentally handicapped will face involuntary sterilization. It is generally accepted that to force a transfusion on an adult Jehovah's Witness is a trespass against him despite the fact that many people regard the Witnesses' prohibition on transfusions as 'irrational'. Any attempt to provide that treatment refusals by *any* group of patients may be overridden requires us to look more closely at the several functions of consent to medical treatment.

THE FUNCTIONS OF CONSENT TO MEDICAL TREATMENT

At one level it might be said that consent to medical treatment involving physical contact is required solely to prevent that contact constituting the tort of trespass to the person. It is simply an application of the general legal principles relating to bodily contact. But in a broader context, consent is seen to serve several functions in medical treatment and research, which perhaps explains why consent to treatment generates so much litigation at a time when generally consent to bodily contact rarely troubles the courts of justice.

What are the functions of consent?

1 Requiring consent affirms and safeguards the patient's autonomy.
2 Consent makes manifest respect for persons.
3 Informed participation in health care may assist and enhance the quality of that care.
4 Requiring consent from patients and research subjects operates as a means of regulating medical practice and research and of preventing abuses.

Examining these functions of consent may help to identify circumstances in which treatment refusals may properly be overridden. Taking autonomy, first, there are arguments from moral philosophy which could be used to justify refusing to act on treatment refusals in the examples discussed in the previous section. If the patient cannot comprehend fully or recall accurately the implications, risks and benefits of what is proposed to him it might be argued that he is unable to exercise true autonomy.[28] Such arguments would necessarily lead to setting the criteria for competence at a much higher level. Rather than the patient needing to understand only the nature and purpose of treatment, she would need to be capable of evaluating the comparative risks, benefits and pains of treatment. Such criteria might render a high percentage of the 'normal' population incompetent. Leaving criteria for competence at a minimal level, distinctions between true autonomy and current preferences might be used to overrule treatment refusals such as that by an elderly patient terrified that having her rotten tooth out will hurt. By giving in to her current preference her autonomy is diminished rather than enhanced. Her decision to refuse treatment on the basis of an 'irrational' fear is, as Richard Lindley terms it, conatively heteronomous, not truly autonomous.[29]

Arguments centred on current preferences versus true autonomy have some attractions. But what are the practical implications of such an approach given legal force? How is the judgment on current preference versus true autonomy to be made? And once again will only patients labelled as abnormal be subjected to forcible enhancement of their 'true autonomy'? Nevertheless one pattern based on such an approach was to be found in the draft version of the Code of Practice[30] to the Mental Health Act 1983.

It was suggested that where a patient refused treatment for a physical condition, treatment might properly be imposed on him if the treatment refusal was a 'result of his mental disorder'. But if his refusal was motivated by some other cause, for instance, religious or cultural convictions, imposition of treatment would be improper. Thus if the patient acted 'against his interests' because of handicap, illness or dementia, his right to decide for himself could be overruled. Should he simply make a decision perceived as unwise or even irrational by his carers, that alone would not justify violating his autonomy.

But can the law really and effectively embody a distinction between true/false autonomy and/or autonomy versus current preferences?

Formidable problems of applying such distinctions will confront us, notably how to judge rationality and irrationality and how to decide when a treatment refusal is motivated by the patient's underlying disorder. None the less, in the context of psychiatric treatment we shall see that Part IV of the Mental Health Act 1983 does attempt such a task. Perhaps similar legislative provision should be made for treatment of physical ills. Would such a pattern meet the needs of the other functions of consent to treatment?

Respect for persons is in this context a two-edged weapon. Do you manifest respect for a mentally handicapped patient more fully by endorsing her limited or distorted decision-making process, or by enhancing her well-being by relieving her of her immediate physical distress. Participation in treatment, the 'therapeutic alliance', may be a more useful guide to what should/may be done to mentally handicapped or disordered patients 'against their will'. If co-operation in treatment is needed to achieve recovery from the physical ill, enforced treatment may end up doing more harm than non-treatment. Even when the immediate aim of relieving the physical disorder is achieved, the trauma of enforced treatment may aggravate the patient's original disorder or dementia. The question of whether treatment may be enforced on the patient becomes one of balancing the advantages and disadvantages of overriding the patient's wishes. This begs the question of *who* can properly make such a judgment.

The House of Lords in *F*[31] assign the judgment in the case of clearly incompetent patients to 'good medical practice'. Entrusting that judgment to the medical profession alone, particularly if it extends beyond indubitably incompetent patients to those whose competence is borderline, entails certain obvious dangers. The final function of patient consent as a means of regulating medical practice and preventing abuse is absent altogether. No one who is not a health care professional reviews the decision of the professional.

Moving on to the thornier problem of research on mentally ill or handicapped patients the test of 'good medical practice' alone is seen as even more inadequate to meet the functions of consent to treatment.[32] If the patient is a pseudo-volunteer, in that the proposed research has no therapeutic benefit for him, no respect for him as a person is manifested by his enforced participation in the project, nor does any mechanism exist formally to protect him from the risks of abuse and exploitation. His only tenuous safeguard, if he is sufficiently aware of what is going on, is to refuse to comply with the procedure. Physical measures to enforce his compliance are, one hopes, unlikely to be resorted to. This offers some inadequate protection against mentally handicapped or disordered patients becoming research subjects 'against their will', but none at all to those patients incapable of expressing what their will may be.

ALTERNATIVE CONSENT PROCEDURES

What alternatives exist to entrusting the decisions on treatment of mentally handicapped and disordered patients entirely to 'good medical practice'? The Mental Health Act 1983 Part IV offers one pattern for safeguards built in to a medical practice model. Consent to psychiatric treatment for mental disorder may be dispensed with subject to special procedures relating to radical or long-term treatment. Section 63 provides that in the case of a patient detained under the Act, the patient's consent is not required for routine treatment 'for mental disorder'. Sections 57 and 58 provide specific safeguards for patients. Briefly, by virtue of section 57[33] any form of psychosurgery and any surgical implant of hormones to reduce male sexual drive is lawful only if

1 the patient is competent to and does give his consent, and
2 such treatment is endorsed by the Mental Health Act Commission.

Section 58 controls the use of electroconvulsive therapy and long-term medication.[34] If the patient is judged to be competent and does consent, his consent must be shown to be 'informed'. If the patient cannot or does not consent, a second opinion doctor appointed by the Mental Health Act Commission must verify that the patient is incapable of or has not consented to the treatment and certify that 'having regard to the likelihood of its alleviating or preventing a deterioration of his condition the treatment should be given'.

The implementation of Part IV of the 1983 Act has by no means been problem free. However, it is at least a coherent attempt to address the problem of consent by mentally disordered patients in a way which actively seeks to balance the rights of patients against their perceived needs, *and* provides for proper scrutiny of medical decision-making. Moreover, unlike any other existing model for substitute consent, Part IV of the Mental Health Act confronts not only the problems of the patient incapable of giving consent, but also the more intractable problem of the patient actively refusing consent.

Unfortunately the Mental Health Act 1983 as it stands is extremely limited in scope. It relates only to treatment for mental disorder and, save for section 57, applies only to that tiny minority of patients formally detained under the Act. The limited scope of the Act leaves the majority of patients in the legal limbo which the courts in *T* v. *T* and *F* v. *West Berkshire Health Authority* have sought to fill. If the patient is incapable of giving consent to treatment, treatment given in her 'best interests' and in conformity with 'good medical practice' is lawful. As a matter of good practice, doctors contemplating irreversible or radical treatment, for example, sterilization, may choose to apply to the courts for a declaration that the proposed treatment is lawful. But they are not obliged to do so.[35]

The unsatisfactory nature of this judicial compromise led WOOD J. in *T* v. *T* to call for the revival of the High Court's *parens patriae* jurisdiction. Under such a jurisdiction mentally handicapped and disordered patients could be made wards of the court so that any necessary non-consensual treatment could be authorized by the court. WOOD J. declared:

> The facts of this case illustrate the usefulness and indeed, may I respectfully suggest, the necessity for a residual jurisdiction even when codification purports to cover every eventuality. The simplest remedy would be to issue a fresh warrant restoring this [*parens patriae*] jurisdiction.[36]

I do not propose to deal here with either the debate on the true nature or historical genesis of the *parens patriae* jurisdiction, nor the dispute on whether it lies dead or merely dormant. All these matters are dealt with by Brenda Hoggett in her masterly essay, 'The royal prerogative in relation to the mentally disordered: resurrection, resuscitation or rejection'.[37] I do endorse WOOD J.'s call for some form of *residual* jurisdiction in the courts. What must be guarded against, however, is the temptation to believe that restoring or creating a jurisdiction enabling judges to consent to treatment on behalf of mentally handicapped or disordered patients solves all the problems created by such patients. First, the role of the court can never be more than residual. Were a High Court judge to be approached every time treatment of an incompetent patient was proposed, the work of the Family Division of the High Court would grind to a halt within a week. The wardship jurisdiction over children, used to adjudicate in disputes over medical treatment of children, is invoked only where the normal mechanism for substitute consent, parental consent, breaks down for some reason. Second, if the residual jurisdiction of the High Court is to operate as a safeguard to a medical practice model (i.e. 'difficult' cases mandatorily require judicial authorization), is it the best means of safeguarding patients' interests? Is a Family Court judge sitting alone equipped to review the initial decision of the health care professionals effectively? Would a statutory procedure for external regulation of decisions to treat mentally handicapped or disordered patients, akin to that already existing in Part IV of the Mental Health Act 1983 in the context of psychiatric treatment, perhaps be more effective? In any case the circumstances in which external authorization of non-consensual treatment was required would have to be clearly defined. Simply restoring *parens patriae* jurisdiction with no criteria for when it must be invoked would be likely to lead to its use in cases where doctors had doubts about treatment or feared a later attack on their decisions, rather than creating any systematic means for protecting patients.

PROXY CONSENT/ADULT GUARDIANSHIP

If the jurisdiction of the court can in practice never be anything but a residual jurisdiction, a superficially attractive solution to 'routine' problems of consent is to give legal force to proxy consent by carers, to establish some form of 'adult guardianship'. A parent would be legally entitled to authorize treatment of her mentally handicapped adult daughter just as she could before that daughter's eighteenth birthday. It does seem ludicrous that if a mentally handicapped girl in the care of her parents needs, for example, a D & C for heavy periods when she is 17½, her parents may lawfully authorize surgery. But if she is 18 and a day they cannot. In practice, doctors may still ask them to sign a consent form on the girl's behalf. In law, that form is meaningless. And the new guidelines on consent to treatment issued by the Department of Health recognize that fact and recommend that relatives and carers be informed about treatment proposals, but not asked to give formal consent.

So why not amend the law to bring it in line with 'reality'? A family member or carer should be able to act as the patient's proxy and authorize treatment in her 'best interests' just as parents do for their children. Several arguments support such a proposal in the context of parents caring for mentally handicapped offspring. The parent knows the patient better than anyone else, can assess her likes and dislikes, and will have her interests at heart. If the patient cannot act for herself, the parent may be seen as the best substitute to carry out on her behalf the various functions of consent. The parent can affirm what limited autonomy the patient enjoys. Because of her intimate knowledge of the patient she is more able to act on the substituted, subjective judgement of the patient rather than the more remote, objective 'best interests' test. She will, because of her care and affection for the patient, seek to manifest respect for her. She can enhance the quality of care by herself participating in treatment of her daughter and by encouraging the patient to co-operate. She will be vigilant against abuse of her child.

All these statements may often be true of parents consenting on behalf of mentally handicapped offspring, parents in the unhappy position of the mother of *T*. But even in such cases there is an inescapable risk that the interest of the proxy may conflict with the interests of the patient. Consider the question of whether or not a mother should authorize sterilization of her mentally handicapped daughter. The mother will necessarily want to do all that she can to avoid adding to her care of her daughter the care of a grandchild. A parent coping with an adult daughter whose handicap is such that she is incontinent and still wears nappies faces a gruesome task each month when the daughter menstruates. Who could blame such a parent if he agreed to a proposal that his daughter be sterilized by hysterectomy? Yet such a decision would be difficult to justify in the interests of the girl herself.

Again and again judges have declared in cases relating to mentally handicapped patients that it is the 'best interests' of the patient, and the patient alone, which must determine what may be done for her. But can this be more than a pious fiction? If a 20-year-old woman is totally incapable of caring for herself and needs parental care for every bodily function, the issue may ultimately become brutally simple. Is she better off without her uterus but with her family, or with her uterus and in an institution because her parents can no longer cope? If we are to give legal powers of proxy consent to family members caring for adult mentally handicapped and disordered patients we must accept that the interests of the carers can never be totally excluded from the decision-making process. If the risk that carers will routinely put their interests above those of the patient is considered too high, then proposals for legal recognition of proxy consent must be abandoned.

Where the proxy is a parent who is in reality simply continuing to fulfil the parental role beyond the age of majority, the risk of conflict of interests may be acceptable. It may indeed even be a false conflict in that the well-being of the parent is so essential to the welfare of the patient that their interests cannot realistically be separated out. But in other relationships and other scenarios the risk of conflict of interests becomes more acute. Consider this hypothetical example. A daughter, herself approaching 60, is asked to consent to her mother, aged 84 and suffering from Alzheimer's Disease, participating in a clinical trial. Mother will be admitted to hospital for two weeks where various tests will be carried out to evaluate the efficacy and safety of a new drug. Offered two weeks of respite from caring for mother, will the proxy be tempted not to scrutinize too carefully what is to be done to the patient?

A vital distinction, of course, between the example of sterilization and the handicapped daughter and this latter example is that the elderly mother is to be enrolled in a research project. Perhaps the powers of any proxy should be limited to powers to consent to treatment of therapeutic benefit to the patient. On analogy with the legal principle governing parental powers, the proxy's powers to consent to the patient's participation in non-therapeutic research might be confined to procedures not *against* the interests of the patient and where any risk to the patient is negligible. How far such a limitation would impede research into, for example, Alzheimer's Disease, would need to be evaluated.

More awkward though than the potential conflict of interest between proxy and patient is the question of where in many cases can you find an appropriate proxy? The 19-year-old girl may remain in the care of her mother who has looked after her from birth. Most older, mentally handicapped and disordered patients are not being cared for by one close family member. They live in an institution or alone in the community until admission to hospital with the physical ailment requiring treatment. If they have little if any contact with their families, there seems little justification for saying the fact that Z is in law the patient's next of kin fits him to act as the patient's proxy. If he has little contact with the patient, he can scarcely fulfil on the patient's behalf the functions of consent discussed earlier.

The most likely proxy thus becomes the patient's social worker and/or the mental handicap team leader responsible for his overall care. The kind of conflict of interests that may arise between family members is unlikely to surface in such cases. But can such a proxy truly act for the patient? Can he really 'stand in the patient's shoes'? At present the medical team treating the patient's current complaint must decide what is to be done in his 'best interests'. Would a proxy in the person of the patient's social worker or mental handicap team leader do this task better? With luck they would have a more intimate knowledge of the patient than the professionals who happen to be called in to deal with the patient's current problem. And their previous contact with and care for the patient would enhance the chance that they will be able to encourage that patient to co-operate in treatment, and where possible enhance his autonomy by seeking to see how far the patient remains able to give his own consent to treatment. None the less in such cases the line between a true patient proxy and a patient advocate becomes a very thin line.

WHAT CAN BE DONE?

Unhappily there does not seem to be any obvious and simple solution to the question of consent to the treatment of mentally handicapped and disordered patients. It is temptingly easy to condemn the current state of affairs where in effect the doctor treating the patient acts as the patient's proxy, and authorizes the treatment which she has proposed. But once alternative procedures to this medical practice model are canvassed they too have innate flaws. Restoration of the *parens patriae* jurisdiction can never be more than a partial solution operating as a 'fail safe' mechanism in controversial cases. The court's jurisdiction must be the icing on the cake with some other principle providing the general everyday rule.

Perhaps what is needed, though, in determining what that rule should be is further consideration of two matters which have as yet received little attention from lawyers.

1 What are the criteria by which we determine competence to consent?
2 When, if at all, may a competent patient's refusal of treatment be overruled?

Only with the answers to those questions can the scale of the problem be evaluated and the categories of patients who cannot authorize their own treatment be settled.

Moving on to the next stage of the process there seem to be two alternative strategies. The current medical practice model could be retained but with safeguards for patients established in that certain procedures would require independent authorization. This could be by way of application to the court under a renewed *parens patriae* jurisdiction or following the pattern of the Mental Health Act 1983 by way of review by independent medical practitioners under the supervision and jurisdiction of the Mental Health Act Commission. Alternatively legal force could be given to proxy consent via adult guardianship with the High Court under a *parens patriae* jurisdiction acting, as it does in the cases of children, as a means of reviewing and challenging the judgement of the proxy. Careful thought would have to be given to who acts as a proxy. Close family members may be in the best position to judge the desires and interests of the patient, but will also be the most likely victims of a conflict of interests with the patient. 'Professional' proxies may be able to evaluate the patient's interests impartially, but know little of what she is able to enjoy and appreciate in her life. Obviously with certain groups of incompetent patients, those who become incompetent through age, disease or accident, consideration must be given to means by which a patient, in advance of the onset of incompetence, can select his own health care proxy. The Durable Power of Attorney for Health Care Act in California offers a model for such a scheme.[38]

Whichever strategy is chosen for substitute consent for incompetent patients, a revised medical practice model or some form of proxy consent/adult guardianship model, the pious fiction of the 'best interests' tests must be reviewed. Individuals exist in society. The more dependent the individual the greater the responsibility society bears for her care. If that responsibility is delegated to a father or a daughter struggling alone with a handicapped child or parent, can society legitimately demand that the carer's interests be disregarded? The now extensive case law on sterilizing mentally handicapped women declares that only the interests of the woman herself should be considered. But can/should we ignore the interests of the child such a woman might bear? If a mentally handicapped woman is sterilized to 'save' her from the risk of pregnancy, in what way does she actually benefit from that surgery? As Heather Draper argues, many ills other than pregnancy ensue from exploitative sexual intercourse.[39] As Peter Mittler cogently points out, a right to sexuality is not ensured by coerced infertility, but by ensuring the privacy and circumstances in which the woman might be enabled to enjoy a sexual relationship.[40] As the Law Commission reviews the law relating to mentally incapacitated patients,[41] their thorniest task is to decide whether the time has come to recognize that 'best interests' is a test more honoured in the letter than the spirit. And then the Commissioners must determine whether to retain that test, and give it substance, or openly accept that other interests may on occasion be valid criteria on which to base decisions about treatment of those who cannot decide for themselves.

Alas, whatever lawyers may propose, the legal rules for treating incompetent patients remain but the tip of the iceberg. How far the rights of people with mental handicap or illness enjoy full recognition and practical respect depends far more on how far non-handicapped people are prepared to welcome the handicapped as fellow members of society, and how far that society is prepared to fund proper facilities for the handicapped, than on anything the law may declare.

NOTES

1 [1984] 3 All E.R. 374 at 378.
2 (1980) *Current Law* 7: 44.
3 See *Wilson* v. *Pringle* [1986] 2 All E.R. 440 at 447.
4 *Re B (A Minor) (Wardship: Sterilisation)* [1987] 2 All E.R. 206 H.L.; *T* v. *T* [1988] 1 All E.R. 613; *F* v. *West Berkshire Health Authority* [1989] 2 All E.R. 545 H.L.; *Re M (A Minor) (Wardship: Sterilisation)* [1988] 2 F.L.R. 497; *Re P (A Minor) (Wardship: Sterilisation)* [1989] 1 F.L.R. 182.
5 Contrast the approach of the Canadian Supreme Court which held that non-therapeutic sterilization would *never* be in the 'best interests' of a mentally handicapped patient; *Re Eve* [1986] 31 D.L.R. (4th) 1.
6 [1989] 2 All E.R. 545 at 551.
7 *Bolam* v. *Friern Hospital Management Committee* [1957] 1 W.L.R. 582.
8 For criticism of the use of the *Bolam* test in this context see M. A. Jones (1989) 'Justifying medical treatment without consent', *Professional Negligence* 5: 178.
9 *Re B (A Minor) (Wardship: Sterilisation)* [1987] 2 All E.R. 206 H.L.
10 *T* v. *T* [1988] 1 All E.R. 613.
11 *F* v. *West Berkshire Health Authority* [1989] 2 All E.R. 545.
12 *T* v. *T* [1988] 1 All E.R. 613.
13 *Re B (A Minor) (Wardship: Sterilisation)* [1987] 2 All E.R. 206 H.L.
14 *F* v. *West Berkshire Health Authority* [1989] 2 All E.R. 545.
15 *Re P (A Minor) (Wardship: Sterilisation)* [1989] 1 F.L.R. 182; and see M. Brazier (1990) 'Sterilisation: down the slippery slope?', *Professional Negligence* 6: 25.
16 [1981] Q.B. 432.
17 See *Sidaway* v. *Board of Governors of the Bethlem Royal Hospital and the Maudsley Hospital* [1985] A.C. 871; see Richard Lindley, Chapter 9 in this volume.
18 [1986] A.C. 151 H.L.

19 Per Lord Scarman, p. 186.
20 Per Lord Scarman, p. 186.
21 [1954] p. 112.
22 See *Williams' The Law Relating to Wills* (1980, 5th edn) ch. 4.
23 *Banks* v. *Goodfellow* (1870) L.R. 5 Q.B. 549.
24 *In the Estate of Holtam* (1913) 108 L.T. 732.
25 *Cleare* v. *Cleare* (1896) L.R. I P & D. 655.
26 [1989] 2 All E.R. 545.
27 See per Lord Brandon, p. 551, and per Lord Griffiths, p. 561.
28 See John Harris (1985) *The Value of Life*, London: Routledge & Kegan Paul, pp. 195–203.
29 See Richard Lindley, Chapter 9 in this volume; and see Harris (1985), op. cit.
30 On p. 89. This section does not appear in the final version of the Code of Practice.
31 [1989] 2 All E.R. 545.
32 The judgments in *F* v. *West Berkshire Health Authority* make no express reference to the problems of the use of mentally handicapped patients in clinical research.
33 Section 57 applies to voluntary patients and patients in the community as well as to detained patients.
34 The administration of any medicine for a period exceeding three months.
35 See *F* v. *West Berkshire Health Authority* [1989] 2 All E.R. 545 at 556–60. And see *J* v. *C (Note)* [1990] 3 All E.R. 735 and *Practice Note (Official Solicitor: Sterilization)* [1990] NLJR 1273. And see also *Re G (Mental Patient: Termination of Pregnancy)*, *The Times* 3 January 1991; *Re E (A Minor)*, *The Times*, 22 February 1991.
36 *T* v. *T* [1988] 1 All E.R. 613, 618.
37 In M. D. A. Freeman (ed.) (1988) *Medicine, Ethics and Law*, London: Sweet & Maxwell, pp. 85–103.
38 See further Age Concern and Centre of Medical Law and Ethics (1988) *The Living Will: Consent to Treatment at the End of Life*, London: Edward Arnold.
39 See Heather Draper, Chapter 6 in this volume.
40 See Peter Mittler, Chapter 3 in this volume.
41 See their excellent and informative consultation document *Mentally Incapacitated Adults and Decision-making: An Overview*, Law Com. Consultation Paper No. 119 (1991) HMSO.

RESEARCH ON THE VULNERABLE

An ethical overview

Raanan Gillon

All the medico-moral problems of ordinary medical practice arise
in the context of medical practice with children and others who
are particularly vulnerable by virtue of their inability adequately
to consider their situations and decide whether or not to take their
doctors' advice. The same applies to medical research. Thus in trying
to analyse the problems of medical research in the special context of
children and other inadequately autonomous people it is important
first to recall the analysis of the ordinary cases. In doing so I have
found the simple analytic framework offered by Beauchamp and
Childress of great value:[1] what are our obligations in terms of
benefiting others, of not harming them, of respecting them as
autonomous agents, and of behaving justly or fairly, whether in
the context of respecting people's rights, distributing inadequate
resources or obeying morally acceptable laws? That framework
plus a consideration of the scope of application of each of these
prima facie principles is compatible with any moral political or
moral philosophical system that I have yet encountered and thus
highly attractive for applied ethics.

THE THERAPEUTIC INTENT AND RELATIONSHIP

In medicine what might be called the standard moral objective is
to produce for one's patient medical benefit with as little harm
as possible – the therapeutic intent specified in the Hippocratic
oath.[2] There is always – or at least almost always – some risk
of harm associated with any medical intervention but that risk, if

it is anything greater than negligible, is justified, in the standard doctor–patient context, if (and I would add only if) the doctor has adequate reason to believe that the probable outcome will be to produce overall net medical benefit for that patient. Moreover, those risks are only to be inflicted if there is adequate reason to believe that the patient or a proper proxy accepts or would accept those risks. I believe those assumptions form part of the normal, therapeutic, doctor–patient relationship.

In order to produce medical benefits for patients, research into what sorts of interventions do so *must* – in some sense of 'research' – have been performed; and in so far as medical interventions on existing patients need improvement further research *must* be done. Part of contemporary medical research is aimed at precisely that objective – to provide the patient who is the subject of that research with the optimal medical treatment. However, medical research is also carried out with a different moral objective, namely to benefit other people than the subject, notably patients of the future. The most obvious example of such research is that carried out on normal volunteers. When doctors do that sort of research they are, I argue, moving away from the central norm of helping the particular patient, and thus away from the norms and assumptions underlying the normal therapeutic relationship between doctor and patient, towards doing something in the general interest, or in the interests of a particular sector of the general body. There is nothing wrong in doing this and indeed it may be highly admirable, but if deceit is to be avoided it must be made clear to the patient that the normal therapeutic doctor–patient relationship either does not exist or has been modified to include objectives that may compete with the patient's best medical interests. Without such information the patient will understandably assume that the normal therapeutic doctor–patient relationship does exist and will base his or her approach upon that assumption. Such an approach will often include a *trust* in the doctor – a trust that whatever the doctor proposes is intended (and intended on the basis of adequate justification) to benefit that patient. Thus when that normal therapeutic assumption does not pertain it is morally essential to make that clear to the patient, and negotiate a new 'contract' based on some other assumptions. If the doctor does not do so, he or she in effect deceives the patient, by trading on the normal therapeutic relationship and its assumptions even though these no longer apply. To avoid such deceit the patient must be informed of the change in relationship and his or her participation sought.

Perhaps an analogy will make this clear. Imagine a home-help going to help an old lady with her domestic chores – that is her job. However, she is also a collector for cancer research. Both are admirable activities but were the home-help to go into the old lady's house in order to do the chores and then while there pop a coin she found on the mantelpiece straight into her collecting tin for cancer research *without asking the old lady*, then we would have not the slightest hesitation in saying she had done wrong (even if the old lady never found out!). Similarly a doctor who did non-therapeutic research on a patient without that patient's adequately informed consent would also be doing wrong; that is why the consent requirements are so much more explicit in the context of non-therapeutic medical research than they are in ordinary therapy, where the patient can rely on the doctor's therapeutic intention and thus, if he so chooses, relax his guard when agreeing to what the doctor proposes ('Oh well the doctor must think it will do me good').

Some medical research is unequivocally therapeutic and designed as part of the standard medical enterprise of benefiting that particular patient. When for example it is not clear which of two standard treatments will be better for a particular patient then it is surely part of that patient's medical care to try and find out which is better, and to do so by the most effective method available. Generally speaking modern methods of clinical research provide more effective ways of deciding such questions than do the traditional but often inadequate method of clinical observation and impression. If the doctor is genuinely agnostic about which of two treatments would be better for her patient then research to find out is part of the normal therapeutic enterprise premised on the normal therapeutic intention of providing medical benefit for the particular patient with minimal harm. Such situations still require adequately informed consent but the norms for adequacy of such consent need be no more stringent than are the norms for ordinary treatment; thus in *such contexts* I agree with Ian Chalmers and Michael Baum, who attack the notion of a 'double standard' for consent in research and in therapy.[3] On the other hand (as indicated above) there is a crucial moral need for a 'double standard' as between treatment and non-therapeutic medical research. Whereas implied consent based on the therapeutic assumption is in many cases justified in ordinary medical treatment, it cannot be justified in non-therapeutic research where the protection for the patient of the doctor's therapeutic intent is by definition absent or reduced and the patient needs to be told explicitly about the intention, risks and benefits of the proposed research and to give his or her explicit consent to participate. However, much clinical research is at neither pole of the spectrum between therapeutic and non-therapeutic research but somewhere in between, sharing both some intention to benefit the subjects of that research and some intention to benefit others by the development of new treatments. Alas, I do not think there is any straightforward or simple method for assessing the balance;[4] I can say only that the closer the project is to the treatment or therapeutic end of the spectrum, with the adequately founded intention of benefiting the subject-patient, the more the normal therapeutic doctor–patient relationship pertains, along with its assumptions. The less there is an intention and probability of benefiting the patient-subject of the research, and the more the research is intended to benefit other patients in the future, so the less of an ordinary therapeutic medical relationship there is and the more important it becomes to explain this to the patient and obtain his or her explicit and informed consent to participation.

CHILDREN, AUTONOMY AND RESEARCH

All this relates to the ordinary situation where the subjects of research are adult autonomous agents. But the normal situation can shed light on the abnormal one in medical ethics as in other aspects of medicine, and the proper treatment of adults can shed light on the proper treatment of children. Children are 'abnormal' in the context of ethical analysis in so far as many are not autonomous at all (think of a 3-month-old baby) so that one cannot respect their autonomy; many others though autonomous are not *sufficiently* autonomous for their autonomy to be respected where such respect would result in harm for the child or would even merely prevent one from doing what is best for the child. (Think of the child who refuses an injection for her meningitis because she does not like the pain of the injection or the child who does not want to go to school because he finds lying in bed watching television more interesting.)

Autonomy, literally self-rule but I think better summarized as deliberated self-rule (or self-determination as the lawyers tend to call it), is a morally crucial capacity and involves the capacities to assimilate adequate information, to deliberate or reflect on the basis of that information, to make a decision based on that deliberation and in some circumstances to act on that decision. The decision-making capacity requires adequate will-power, a point of particular relevance in psychiatric practice, where some patients, whether mentally ill or suffering from a mental disability, may have the capacities to acquire information and deliberate but not have sufficient will-power to make or enact decisions. I suspect that adequate will-power includes the capacity to override immediate impulses in order to achieve deliberated longer-term objectives, in which case it is also of particular relevance to the question of adequate autonomy in children. If any of these features of autonomous intentional action (including mental action) is *sufficiently* diminished or absent the requirement to respect autonomy may be overridden in order to benefit and/or to prevent harm to the subject – and once again where the features of autonomy are totally absent it is simply impossible to respect autonomy (though sometimes previously expressed autonomous decisions are known and can be respected).

A PITFALL

There is a potentially worrying problem here, exemplified by Komrad,[5] who argues explicitly that if our aim in medicine is to maximize our patients' autonomy then it may be permissible and indeed morally required to override such autonomy as they have in order to increase it. Thus according to Komrad's arguments if a patient, otherwise well and autonomous, has some phobia that results in his rejecting a treatment needed to overcome that phobia it is part of our duty as doctors to override his rejection and treat the patient so as to maximize his autonomy by ridding him of the phobia. Apart from slippery-slope worries (any illness entails *some* reduction in autonomy, so by parity of reasoning any refusal of treatment should be overridden by doctors so as to increase the patient's autonomy) the argument trades on a conflation of *respect* for autonomy and *maximization* of autonomy. To respect a person's autonomy is to respect her autonomous choices, even those that reduce her subsequent autonomy; thus a person may autonomously decline medical treatment that would prolong her life, and so reduce or even totally eliminate her subsequent autonomy (assuming that one is not autonomous after one is dead) but the obligation to respect autonomy (that is to respect the patient's deliberated choices) requires the doctor to refrain from treatment. Conversely were the obligation really to *maximize* autonomy then Komrad could be correct.

While I realize that this is to give short shrift to a complex argument, let me simply here assert that the proper understanding of respect for autonomy, and the understanding that exists in our society, is respect for people's deliberated choices, *not* maximization of autonomy. If doctors wish to use the maximization objective they must first argue for it and persuade their societies, or at least their patients, that they are right in this interpretation. They must not simply impose it. Meanwhile we owe respect for people's adequately deliberated choices (in so far as it is compatible with equal respect for the autonomy of all affected) to all who are themselves *adequately*, rather than maximally, autonomous.

AGE AND ADEQUATE AUTONOMY OR 'MATURITY' OR 'COMPETENCE'

In our society adequate autonomy is assumed to exist by the time a person reaches adulthood at 18 years of age, at which time people's decisions about how to rule their own lives are normally legally respected unless they infringe the autonomy of others or harm others.[6] In the context of health care a person's decisions are normally respected on reaching the age of 16, when for example a person may legally consent to medical treatment.[7] These ages are only presumptive and if evidence exists that the person is not adequately autonomous or 'mature' or 'competent' (both of which in this context amount to much the same idea as adequately autonomous) then the presumption may be overridden, for example by making a child a ward of court, or by compulsory treatment under the Mental Health Act 1983 of adults who are sufficiently mentally ill not to be adequately autonomous and who are a danger to themselves or to others.[8]

While above certain legally specified ages one is presumed to be competent (sufficiently autonomous) to make one's own decisions, below those ages one is presumed *not* to be so competent and below these ages if people's decisions are deemed to be against their interests either by harming them or by failing to benefit them sufficiently then those decisions may properly and legally be overridden by those who have responsibility for their care. In our society, and in most societies, it is the parents who are given the duty of care for their children, on the grounds that they are the most likely to promote the 'best interests' of those children. Thus it is parents who normally give legal consent for medical treatment of children under 16, who are their proxies so far as respect for autonomy is concerned. However, age is only a rough indicator of maturity, competence or adequate autonomy and fairly recent developments in the law have, I think, made this clearer. Thus while 16 remains the presumptive age at which a child can give legal consent for medical treatment, the House of Lords' decision in the *Gillick* case[9] allows a doctor to accept the independent consent to treatment of a younger child provided the child shows that he or she is sufficiently competent or mature to make such decisions – in my terminology by showing that he or she is adequately autonomous to have such decisions respected.

Thus in the context of ordinary medical treatment children below the age of 16 are presumed in English law not to be adequately autonomous to make their own treatment decisions and their parents are charged with the responsibility for making treatment decisions on their behalf, but if a doctor has reason to believe that the child younger than 16 *is* adequately competent to make such decisions, and if despite strenuous efforts to persuade the child to involve the parents such involvement is refused, and if the doctor believes the treatment to be in the child's interests, then he or she may prescribe such treatment without consulting or even informing the parents. A second type of situation in which the parents' role as proxies for their children may be overridden is when they are deemed not to be acting in their child's interests. This requires a court's decision, as for example when a child is made a ward of court. In such circumstances the duty of care devolves upon the appointed guardian, who will be responsible for, among other things, giving consent for medical treatment of the child.

DISAGREEMENT BETWEEN DOCTORS AND PROXIES

What about cases where the doctor and parents (or guardians) disagree about a child's medical treatment? Of course the usual procedure is for the doctor to explain why he or she thinks a certain course of treatment is in the child's interests and try to persuade the parents to agree. But if the parents disagree it is possible for the doctor to take one of at least three courses of action: to accept the parents' or guardians' decision, to impose the treatment he or she believes to be in the child's interests, or to seek for the child to be made a ward of court on the grounds that the parents are not exercising their duty of care. Generally speaking it seems to me that the morally preferable course of action is to accept the parents' view – on many treatment decisions there are valid differences of opinion and unless there is good reason to believe that the parents' decision is positively and clearly dangerous to the child more harm than good would, I believe, result from rejecting the social structures we have whereby parents are deemed to be the proper proxy decision-makers for their children. However, where the doctor believes that the parents' decision is patently dangerous then it seems he or she has a moral duty – grounded in a duty of beneficence to the child – to try to protect the child from harm. My own preferred approach would be to refer the case to a properly appointed adjudicator to hear both sides of the case and adjudicate. This seems to me not only the fairest way of resolving what is in essence a dispute between carers over what constitutes the best outcome for the child, but also the way justice can most obviously be seen to be done. However, in an emergency it is always open to the doctor to impose life-saving treatment and invite the parent to take him or her to court though – as I understand matters and as a non-lawyer – the parent is unlikely to succeed in such an action. The best known type of case in this context is where Jehovah's Witness parents refuse life-saving blood transfusions for their child. The underlying moral justification for imposition of such life-saving treatment is that in the absence of reliable evidence *from the person concerned* that he or she would prefer to die rather than have a straightforward relatively harmless life-saving treatment, the presumption should be that the person would prefer to stay alive. Of course the question is begged in the phrase 'relatively harmless', for Jehovah's Witnesses believe that *eternal* harm results from having a blood transfusion – but again the justification for overriding *their* beliefs is that without reliable evidence that the person concerned (the child) autonomously shares these very unusual views the assumption should be that the child would prefer to remain alive on Earth.

Thus far, therefore, I have argued that parents are the normal, socially approved and proper proxy decision-makers for their inadequately autonomous children, and indeed have certain rights as such, but that these rights are derived from a proper and socially approved duty of care by parents for their children; thus where there is clear evidence of failure in the parental duty of care, due process can properly be instituted to withdraw those rights of proxy decision-making. And in a life-threatening emergency the due process may properly come after someone else, including a doctor, has imposed life-saving measures against the will of the parents, though it is always preferable in justice for the due process to come before the decision to impose life-saving treatment is enacted, if this is possible.

MEDICAL RESEARCH ON CHILDREN

How do these various considerations help us in the context of medical research on children? First, the distinction between therapeutic and non-therapeutic research is an important one. In so far as the research project is therapeutic, that is as indicated above, intended with reasonable likelihood of success medically to benefit the child who is the subject (for instance a comparison of two standard treatments for the child's illness, or of a standard treatment against a new treatment which holds out reasonable hope of being a better treatment for the child's illness) then the parents can clearly act in their child's interests in agreeing for the child to be a subject of the research project. At the other non-therapeutic research end of the spectrum the issue is far less clear. Some would hold that parents should in *no* circumstances give permission for their child to be a research subject in non-therapeutic medical research if that carries any risk of harm for the child, no matter how small that risk of harm may be – indeed that was the gist of the legal opinion given to the Medical Research Council on the subject.[10] Even a one-in-a-million chance that the child will be seriously harmed by participation should, so such people argue, be sufficient to prevent parents giving consent for the child's participation as a subject. Moreover, the argument may proceed, even if the parents consent to such participation and even if law permits it, doctors should not undertake it, for by their professional ethics they must never impose risk of harm on their patients except where to do so is in the patient's interests or where the risk is small and the patient has consented to bear a risk in the interests of others. And such arguments have impressive back-up, including the authoritative international agreement of the World Medical Association in its Declaration of Helsinki.[11]

Although I sympathize with the motivation of such arguments – after all we do feel and want to feel that parents should deliberately expose their children to risks only if these are in the child's interests, and that of all groups doctors should not aid and abet errant parents who are prepared to expose their children to risks that are *not* in the child's interests – none the less on reflection I think this view, *if taken literally*, is excessively restrictive and inconsistent with our normal moral attitudes to the role of parents in relation to their children, as I now hope to show. Of course to show that a proposal is inconsistent with our current social norms is not to show that it is wrong – it may be that our current norms are wrong; but that would require further argument.

A JUSTIFICATION FOR MINIMAL RISK NON-THERAPEUTIC RESEARCH ON CHILDREN

So how might one begin to justify non-therapeutic research on children unable to give their adequately informed and adequately autonomous consent? By looking, I think, at the norms of permissible risk-infliction by parents on their children in our society and at the implications for those norms of the moral claim that underpins the argument forbidding *all* non-therapeutic research on children, no matter how small the risk. Thus in our society, and in all that I know about, parents are permitted to impose a certain degree of risk on their children even though that risk is not in the child's interests. Moreover, we allow parents to impose such risks either in order to benefit others, or, if the risk is sufficiently small, simply because it is convenient for the parents! Well, it might be argued in immediate response, if that is the case it ought not to be the case, and the standards being urged for non-therapeutic research should be applied to all cases in which parents are imposing risks on their children that are not in the children's interests. But let us consider some cases. First, cases where the risk is imposed on the child in order to benefit someone else. Imagine a parent taking a child in a car to visit grandmother in hospital, or to take an injured friend to hospital; or simply for a ride in the country or to the seaside when the rest of the family wish to go but the child concerned wants to stay at home. To take a child for a car ride is indisputably to impose a risk of harm on that child, indeed a possible risk of very severe harm, even of death. In the examples offered that risk of harm would be imposed in the interests of others and not in the interests of the child. The moral standard set by those who would ban all non-therapeutic research, no matter how small the risk to the child, would also ban such car rides except where these were in the interests of the child. Imagine another example: a child gate blocks the top of the stairs so as to reduce the risk of the child falling down the stairs. At some stage the gate is to be taken away – after all Henrietta is soon to be 5 and perhaps it is time for her to learn to cope with the stairs unprotected by the gate. Then the local day nursery asks for a child gate and Henrietta's parents, somewhat against the judgement of her mother, decide to donate Henrietta's child gate which after all will protect more and younger and therefore more vulnerable children. The next day Henrietta, who always was an awkward little girl, falls down the newly unprotected stairs and is admitted to hospital with concussion. Well of course the latter case just goes to show that the parents were wrong to take away the gate and give it to the day nursery, does it not? And does the same not apply to the car examples. If an accident *had* occurred and the child *had* been injured that would have been the direct result of the decision to take the car ride. So of course the parents ought not to have taken the child for the car ride, ought they? Then imagine similar examples where the benefit was merely the parent's own convenience ('I'm fed up with all the fiddle of this wretched child gate – she's old enough to learn to cope with the stairs and I'm taking it down NOW' or 'We're going out for a drive because I *feel* like going out for a drive – so stop whingeing and get into the car'). Well, *would* the parent be wrong in those cases to impose that extra risk on the child simply for the parent's own benefit or convenience?

My own belief is that such imaginary but plausible examples show that on reflection we – the social we – do accept that parents may impose a certain level of risk on their children and that though we are more inclined to justify such risk where it is imposed for the benefit of others, none the less at *some very low level of risk* we also would justify such risk-imposition simply for the benefit or convenience of the parents. If this is so and if after reflection we accept as justified such low-risk imposition in ordinary life by parents on their children why should we not also allow it in the context of equally low-risk activities involving non-therapeutic medical research? My own belief is that we should, provided:

1 that the research has some reasonable prospect of benefiting others (that is it is not merely for the convenience of parents or doctors)
2 that the research imposes no greater than very low risk of harm, equivalent to or less than the ordinary risks that we properly allow parents to impose on their children in ordinary life, and acceptable within the bounds of their acknowledged duty of care for their children
3 that the parents as the child's proper proxies have given properly informed consent
4 that the research has been authorized by a bona fide ethics committee.

Of course we then face the undeniably difficult task of trying to define what sorts of specific activities in non-therapeutic medical research are of sufficiently low risk and of sufficiently probable benefit to others to fall within those criteria. That is a matter for thorough analysis both in general terms (the Institute of Medical Ethics Working Party's Report edited by Dr Richard Nicholson attempted to do this, and he expands on that discussion in Chapter 2 of this volume)[12] and in the context of ethics committees' deliberations about specific research proposals. Such deliberations are helped by empirical studies of the actual effects of particular types of non-therapeutic intervention, for example, the study of the effects on children of having their blood taken in order to benefit others.[13]

The only general points perhaps worth adding in the context of such analyses is that whenever harms and benefits are being assessed it is important to try to differentiate their various components, notably *'objective' descriptions* of the harms and benefits (cf pain and discomfort and other possible harms of antecubital venepuncture; development of knowledge of blood levels of various substances in normal children for later comparison with levels in certain groups of sick children); *subjective descriptions* of harms and benefits (cf normal reluctance of children and others to have a needle put into an arm vein compared with terror of such an event in a small minority of children; subjective pleasure at being involved in a special project to help sick children); the *probability* of such harms and benefits (cf a very high probability of the usually minor harm of feeling a needle prick versus a very low probability of developing an infection as a result, and a minuscule probability of the infection actually causing the child's death); and finally *whose* harms and whose benefits? And as argued above such analyses then need to be put into the context of similar analyses for, for example, car drives and other activities that children are routinely and deliberately involved in at the proper and acceptable behest of their parents in ordinary life.

AN ADDITIONAL PROFESSIONAL CONSTRAINT

The defence outlined above for the acceptability of minimal risk non-therapeutic research on children given the informed consent of their parents was based on the general acceptability of a certain low level of risk-imposition by parents on their children in the course of ordinary everyday life. There is, however, another relevant moral concern which should, I argue, limit the level of acceptable risk in non-therapeutic research. This is the level of risk of harm that the medical and other caring professions themselves decide should be an acceptable upper limit of harm that they may properly allow themselves to inflict on their patients as one group and on the subjects of their non-therapeutic research as another group. This upper limit of acceptable harm should certainly be no greater than the level acceptable to the societies in which they practise, but it may quite properly be lower. The underlying argument here is that it is important for the medical profession, which has so much power to harm others, to make it utterly clear to all that it will risk harm, other than the most minimal, only where the intention is to produce net-benefit-over-harm for those potentially harmed. This is, I think, the rationale for contemporary medical standards that prohibit the imposition of risks greater than minimal on any subject of non-therapeutic medical research *even if the subject or the subject's proper proxy were prepared to accept greater risks in the altruistic desire to benefit others.* It is a stance that is compatible with the ancient Hippocratic therapeutic commitment and is justifiable both in terms of the doctor's and the profession's own therapeutic objective of providing medical benefit for the individual patient. It is also justified by a utilitarian concern to maximize social welfare. Thus it seems highly probable to me that if doctors ever started to inflict greater than minimal harm on their patients or subjects in the interests of others, for example to push forward the frontiers of medicine in order to benefit patients in the future – that is if they ever decided to permit substantially risky non-therapeutic medical research – then widespread social concern would be the result. Doctors would be widely distrusted and medical care for the population would suffer catastrophically. So even if, by chance, willing subjects came forward – or willing parents 'volunteered' their children as subjects for non-therapeutic research involving greater than minimal risk, still, I argue, doctors should continue to refuse to carry out such risky non-therapeutic research, regardless of the potential benefit to others in the future that might result from it.

HIGHER RISKS MAY BE JUSTIFIED IN THERAPEUTIC RESEARCH ON CHILDREN

Matters are quite different of course in the context of therapeutic research, where very substantial risks may be justified *provided* the intended and reasonably anticipatable benefit to the patient is greater than the risk. Therapeutic research is research where the intention of the researcher is to provide the best care for the particular patient who is the subject of that research. As I have already suggested a clear example might be where two standard treatments for the subject's condition are being compared and the doctor does not know which is actually more effective. Here the question of risk is approached as in ordinary medical treatment by the criterion of net-benefit-over-harm: is the proposed intervention reasonably anticipated to produce net benefit-over-harm for the patient? In some circumstances the treatment may itself be substantially harmful (think of radical surgery such as an amputation, or of certain kinds of cancer chemotherapies) but the harm risked or inevitable is calculated to be less harmful than continuing with the disease untreated or treated differently. So, for example, while one should not countenance chopping off a leg, or doing a brain biopsy, or administering radiotherapy in healthy volunteers (no matter how beneficial for others the results might be) each of those in themselves harmful treatments might be appropriate for a patient whose life may be saved as a result. And each might be properly carried out in the context of therapeutic research in an effort to ensure the optimal treatment for the patient-subjects of such research. Furthermore, while in adults adequately informed consent would be necessary from the patient-subjects themselves, in the case of children such adequately informed consent should *presumptively*, as argued earlier, be obtained from the child's proxy, normally the parents, in cases where the child is not adequately autonomous to make such decisions himself or herself. (Though it is important to add that while the final decision whether or not to accept a proposed treatment for an 'inadequately autonomous' child should be the parent's or other proper proxy's, first, the implications of the *Gillick* judgment for assessing the competence of children younger than 16 should be recalled – some under-16-year-olds *are* adequately competent, mature or autonomous enough to make their own decisions – and second, even with children who are too immature to make the final decision, it is often highly desirable to involve them in the decision-making processes.)

So far I have discussed the moral issues of research on children in terms of respect for autonomy (with special emphasis on the problems that arise when children are not adequately autonomous for such respect to be a substantial moral concern, and where parents or other proxies have the role of autonomous decision-makers on behalf of the children, as part of their duty of care); of beneficence and non-maleficence (with special differentiation between therapeutic medical research done for the specific benefit of the patient-subjects of that research and non-therapeutic research done for the benefit of others); but I have not said anything about the fourth Beauchamp and Childress principle, justice.

JUSTICE AND RESEARCH ON CHILDREN

As stated, three aspects of justice or fairness can usefully be differentiated; distributive justice or the need to treat people fairly in the context of the distribution of burdens and benefits, including the distribution of scarce beneficial resources; justice as respect for people's rights; and justice as respect for morally acceptable laws.

So far as distributive justice goes, it is I believe important to recall the economists' concept of opportunity cost: every resource used up to benefit Jack and Jill is a resource lost to Tom, Dick and Harry. Of course that is not to say that such a distribution is therefore unfair or unjust to Tom, Dick and Harry, but it is to say that there is a *potential* problem of justice unless the unequal distribution is justified. So *somewhere* along the line, the fairness of the distribution of burdens and benefits in medical research, including especially medical research on those who are less than adequately autonomous to look after their own interests, requires consideration. For example at the national level how much of the overall resources allocated to health care should go into medical research of different kinds, using what criteria of justification and decided by whom? And similarly at the local level, how much of the locally available resources should go into the various types of medical research, using what criteria of justification and decided by whom? This seems to me particularly important in the context of non-therapeutic research, for there the benefits are intended for others in the future – for example future patients who may benefit from any new medications developed as a result of such research – and in so far as the resources for such research come out of a fixed health care budget they necessarily have an opportunity cost so far as resources for those who are currently ill are concerned. I wish I had satisfactory solutions for these problems but I do not; none the less, that they ought to be addressed as part of the ethical analysis seems clear. Just as there is a justice problem in the context of distribution of resources and thus of benefits, so there is in the context of burdens – and suffice it to say that wherever any risk of harm (a burden) is to be imposed on those who are especially vulnerable by virtue of weakness in some sense or another then there is a particular duty on those caring for them to prevent the imposition on them of an unfair or unjust proportion of any burden, including in this context the burdens of being a research subject.

The second aspect of justice is respect for rights. There is of course considerable philosophical debate about the very existence of rights but suffice it to say that in practice almost everyone recognizes that people do have rights, and among these rights are a right not to be physically or psychologically invaded by others, even in the interests of benefiting the community as a whole or some sector of it. This recognition can sometimes underlie the objection discussed above to *any* form of non-therapeutic research on children. It is a powerful moral check on any substantial non-therapeutic medical interference with children but the claim that it would prohibit all such research even where the risk is extremely small can be countered, and I believe successfully countered, with arguments of the kind I have offered above for permitting tightly controlled minimal risk non-therapeutic research on children.

Finally justice requires respect for morally acceptable laws. One has only to think of the laws of regimes one detests as thoroughly immoral to recognize that the qualification morally acceptable is essential. That said one may also decide that if laws have been created in a morally acceptable way – for example by a morally reflective democratic mechanism – then there will be a strong moral presumption that they should be obeyed. Suffice it to say that so far as this non-lawyer is concerned it appears that, as Mason and McCall Smith aver in relation to non-therapeutic research,[14] many of the legal issues concerning research on children remain to be determined by the courts. None the less there is a substantial body of relevant law and chapters in the Institute of Medical Ethics' book on paediatric research,[15] and in medico-legal textbooks by Skegg,[16] Brazier[17] and Kennedy and Grubb.[18] These are instructive and in my view, as indicated, relevant to the ethical analysis of the issues.

AN APPLICATION OF THE MORAL-ANALYTIC FRAMEWORK OUTLINED

To conclude I shall attempt to outline an application of the moral-analytic framework briefly described above to the type of situation confronted in an earlier contribution to this discussion concerning consent for research on the vulnerable, notably to the question of research on newborns who have respiratory distress syndrome (RDS).[19] Consider the following type of case: there are two alternative treatments for RDS, one of which is the standard treatment and the other a non-standard treatment. For good reasons those experienced in the medical care of newborn infants believe that the latter treatment is likely to be better for babies with RDS but they are not sure about this because they do not have strong scientific evidence for their belief of the sort provided by randomized controlled clinical trials (RCTs). In order to try to decide more conclusively which of the two treatments is preferable they set up a research protocol to compare the two treatments. In such a case it seems clear to me that the trial falls into the therapeutic research category with the intention being primarily to benefit the baby subjects of the research (though of course there is, as with all medical research, also the intention to try to obtain generalizable knowledge for the benefit of others). Thus the moral norms of ordinary medical treatment are applicable, based on the ordinary therapeutic assumption that the doctor will try to produce net-benefit-over-harm for the patient being treated. So far as respect for autonomy is concerned, do these norms require adequately informed consent from the infant? Of course not. Do they require adequately informed consent from the infant's proper proxy, who as I indicated earlier would normally be the parents (and perhaps particularly the mother, though that is another moral issue)? As indicated earlier I believe the answer is yes, adequately informed consent is required, but what that amounts to may legitimately vary according to first, the circumstances – emergencies normally call for emergency action – and second, the wishes of the patient, or the patient's proper proxy, for whom, for example, information that the doctors are trying to do their best for the infant may be adequate for some patients and for some parent-proxies, and not at all adequate for others.

So far as the circumstances are concerned clinical treatment decisions for RDS normally have to be taken in an emergency and the opportunity for explanation, discussion of alternatives, deliberation and explicit consent does not exist. In an emergency it is surely proper for doctors to presume consent to treatment that the doctor believes to be potentially life-saving in the absence of very strong reasons to believe the contrary. Imagine a doctor on confronting a cardiac arrest delaying the start of resuscitation in an effort to discuss the pros and cons and obtain consent either from the patient or from the proper proxy. While not usually quite such a rapidly fatal emergency the case of RDS in a newborn infant seems reasonably analogous. That is by no means to say that there are no circumstances in which explicit consent should be obtained in emergencies and it depends very much on the specific circumstances, and whether it is reasonable to ask the mother in those specific circumstances whether she, on behalf of the infant, would prefer treatment *A* or treatment *B*. Among the morally most important variables here will be how dangerous to the life and health of the infant the delay caused by such consultation would be and how reasonable a presumption of consent in those circumstances would be. For example if the non-standard trial treatment involved the use of blood products and the standard treatment did not then the presumption of consent if the parent was a Jehovah's Witness would be quite unreasonable and wrong and the standard treatment should be used in the absence of explicit consent and in the absence of scientifically strong evidence that the blood product would be substantially more likely to save the baby's life. If on the other hand the blood product *was* the standard treatment for saving the child's life then as argued earlier the doctor *might* decide to treat with blood in the emergency, though I believe that wherever possible such a deep conflict over what would be in the child's interests – including what would constitute net-benefit-over-harm for the child – should be adjudicated by a proper court or other quasi-legal body. In this context it would be important in justice to remember that so far as Jehovah's Witness parents are concerned treatment with blood to preserve this earthly life costs the treated person loss of eternal life thereafter and that thus from their perspective they are indeed protecting the interests of their child in refusing blood. While I personally agree with the contemporary legal and medical position in Britain which broadly forbids parents to make such straightforward, and in this life at any rate low-risk, life-denying decisions for their children on the basis of their own metaphysical concerns, I do think that it is fairer and moreover will be seen to be fairer if the conflict is submitted to the judgement of a properly appointed adjudicating authority.

What about the amount of information that ought to be given parents in non-emergency situations? Again the analogy with ordinary treatment seems relevant for trials which are clearly therapeutic – that is with the primary intent and reasonable probability of producing net-benefit-over-harm for the patient. And in ordinary treatment I think the question turns on what would the patient want to know. In my view *most* patients given tactful and sometimes repeated opportunities to learn about their condition and the treatment options do want to know – but some do not want to know nasty medical information about themselves and simply want the doctor to do whatever can be done to make things better. Can this be relevant where proxies are acting for non-autonomous patients? Here it might be argued that the proxy *ought* to be fully informed whether or not the proxy wants to know, on the grounds that it is the proxy's responsibility to act in the interests of the child. But does not the question then turn on whether or not it is possible for a proxy/parent to act in the interests of the child without very much in the way of information other than the basic information that the doctor is going to act to produce net-benefit-over-harm consistent with the standard Hippocratic therapeutic commitment? As a practising doctor I believe that such trust is an entirely morally justifiable stance for a parent and entirely consistent with a parent's duty of care. *And of course the opposite position is just as morally reputable.* So if a parent does want to know all about the proposed therapeutic trial he or she should be given the requested information. If, however, my argument is accepted that information should not be imposed on parents who do not want it in the context of genuinely therapeutic trials involving their children, the corollary must surely be that doctors planning such trials and ethics committees considering them are clearly aware of the moral distinction between therapeutic trials and non-therapeutic trials *and of the spectrum of trials that falls between the polar examples.* The more the trial is non-therapeutic, the less its intention and probability is to benefit the patient-subject, the more imperative it becomes to make clear to the parent/proxy that the trial is not part of the ordinary therapeutic relationship and to solicit explicit and informed consent for incorporating the child into a project that is primarily or entirely designed for the benefit of others.

There remains an important dilemma: suppose the treating doctor has what he or she on reflection and taking into account the inadequacies of the available information believes to be good reason to believe that one treatment is superior to another, even though the two treatments have still not been evaluated by the rigorous science of RCTs. In those circumstances it seems to me that the therapeutic Hippocratic ethos of trying to provide the best available treatment for the individual patient requires that the doctor explain the situation to the parent(s) where this is possible, including the fact that until the scientific evidence of the RCT becomes available the doctor's opinion and preference may well prove wrong and be little if any better than hunch, and then give his opinion as to which is the preferable treatment. A useful guide (no more) in such circumstances would be the doctor's answer to the question, 'Which treatment would I give my own child, or am I really in such a state of "equipoise" that I would be happy to enter my own child into the RCT?' Such an approach may well be rejected by the tough-minded scientist as being based more on uselessly unreliable intuition or sentiment than on real knowledge – indeed I would agree with such a scientist that doctors have a duty to evaluate their reasons for preferring one treatment to the other as rigorously as possible – but I personally believe that in the end the doctor's informed opinion, even when it is not based on the hard scientific evidence of RCTs, is still more likely than not to defend, preserve and promote the interests of his or her patient. So as a practising doctor I would recommend the treatment I genuinely believed to be better. But I would try extremely hard to scrutinize that belief for evidence of gullibility and mere wishful thinking on my part. Imagining myself into the role of medical parent of a newborn baby with RDS I personally would want to know about the trial if possible but I would accept the expert assessment of my baby's doctor and permit the baby being entered into an RCT provided the doctor had no personal belief that one of the treatments was probably more effective than the other – and provided one treatment was not clearly and substantially more distressing or risky than the other.

None the less there are some circumstances in which I know I would part company with the scientists. Some time ago, for example, there was a plan to assess the efficacy of giving pregnant women vitamin B complex so as to try to reduce the incidence of spinal defects in their babies. The preliminary but non-controlled trial evidence of such efficacy was sufficiently plausible to me to ensure that I would never dream of recommending participation in a double-blind placebo-controlled trial to any pregnant woman with a history of having given birth to a baby with spinal cord defects – even though I would fully recognize that my own assessment was based on scientifically inadequate evidence that vitamin B complex was more likely to be beneficial than an inert substance, and I would explain this to the pregnant woman. But I would also recognize and explain the dangers of my adopting this position – notably the very real danger that the preliminary evidence on which I was relying was actually false. After all doctors like me were probably using exactly the same sort of reasoning when they learned from preliminary clinical evidence that 100 per cent oxygen was good for newborn babies born prematurely and administered the oxygen to such babies. Only very much later and after many babies – perhaps 10,000 – became blind from retrolental fibroplasia caused, at least in part, by that oxygen treatment, did scientifically controlled trials begin to show its dangers. And while the early results were simplistically interpreted with an over-reduction in oxygen treatment producing its own harms, the importance of subjecting doctors' clinical impressions to rigorous scientific scrutiny *in the interests of their patients* was unequivocally demonstrated.[20] So in this as in all things a balance between competing claims remains essential!

Finally then, how would consideration of justice issues influence my assessment of the RDS type of therapeutic trial in newborn infants? Well, I would want the cost implications to have been assessed because of the distributive justice opportunity cost implications of, for example, a very expensive new medication for the distribution of medical resources both locally and nationally. I do not think that this assessment is best done by the researching doctor, perhaps not even by the ethics committee, but *somewhere* along the line it should be done both at local level and at national level. The power of medical scientists to produce new and beneficial treatments is an ever-expanding one and I for one am highly optimistic that great advances for the benefit of mankind will continue to be achieved by medical science. But I am also acutely aware that such advances rarely save money (though occasionally they do) and that more and more resources will have to be devoted to medical care if they are to be distributed to all who could benefit. At some stage people who provide those resources will rightly say 'enough' – medical care for all is desirable but so are all sorts of other activities. We need a mechanism for rational assessment of new and potentially costly medical advances, first to ensure that they are indeed beneficial, and second, for deciding how much if any resources to allocate to them *in the context of other competing and perhaps equally or more beneficial activities* both medical and non-medical, health-care and non-health-care orientated.

So far as justice in the context of respect for people's rights is concerned I would simply reiterate under this head the fact that doctors are not allowed to interfere with people without those people's explicit or implicit permission, or the permission of their proper proxies and people have a *right* not to have medical things done to them without their consent or the consent of their proper proxies. While such consent may be properly inferred in certain circumstances especially where attempts to save a person's life are concerned, such inference must be cautiously used especially where the normal therapeutic relationship proffered by doctors to their patients is significantly compromised by non-therapeutic intentions such as medical research done for the benefit of others. However, in the type of trial postulated, comparing RDS treatments in emergency, I would argue as above that explicit consent need not necessarily be obtained provided that the doctor was in 'equipoise' about which treatment was better for the patient. My own preference none the less would be to offer all parents information about the trial even if the offer could be made only retrospectively, after the treatment had been started in emergency.

So far as justice and the law is concerned I generally accept the moral validity of obeying laws in Britain given that they have been arrived at through a morally acceptable democratic process. The law in this context includes explicit prohibition of unconsented to medical interference or indeed any 'touching' as the somewhat quaint legal phraseology has it and that is an important justice-based backdrop to assessment of the proposed clinical trial. However, the law (as I, a non-lawyer, understand it) also sympathetically understands the constraints imposed by emergencies and emergency treatment reasonably intended to save a person's life can usually be legally justified by 'necessity' and/or by the person's presumed consent. Moreover, and again in general terms, the law in Britain places great weight on the medical profession's own reasonable assessments of what amounts to good medical practice. Suffice it to conclude that so far as I am aware, the moral analysis offered earlier is consistent with British law: what I have proposed is not illegal!

Finally, issues of scope have of course arisen in the context of my analysis that apply in the RDS research type of case. Thus I have argued that the scope of the principle of respect for people's autonomy cannot and does not apply to newborn infants and the system of proper proxies is a response to this fact, with parents being presumptively the proper proxies for their children but with that presumption always being open to question if their behaviour indicates that they are failing to protect their child. However, I have argued that such issues should, except in emergencies, be determined through due process. So far as the scope of beneficence and non-maleficence is concerned I have pointed to the difference in scope of the therapeutic concern to benefit preferentially one's particular patient, versus the broader scope of medical science which is concerned to benefit patients and potential patients generally. This difference in scope is of moral relevance in practice in (among other contexts) the context of the difference between therapeutic and non-therapeutic research, and I have argued that clarity about which role the doctor is functioning in (including clarity about when he or she is functioning in both roles) is morally crucial. And I have argued that because people generally and patients in particular assume that when doctors do, or propose to do, things to them these things will be done for their benefit, any significant deviation from this presumption must be explained to the patient or proxy. However, in the context of the proposed RDS therapeutic research such deviation does not seem to be a significant moral issue and the normal therapeutic/Hippocratic assumptions seem to apply. So far as the scope of justice is concerned I have argued that the scope of distributive justice *ought* to be considered for medical research in general and for this sort of trial in particular though (I have suggested but not argued) this probably ought not to be the function of the researching doctor or even the ethics committee. (This is an area where far more work and thought are needed!) I did not discuss the scope of justice in the context of rights and in the context of law, merely implying that I was limiting their scope to people in Britain – there are of course deep and contentious moral issues buried in that limitation.

This has been a long and for non-philosophers relatively complex analysis (though as usual I suspect not complex enough for some philosophers). In it I have tried to explore some of the conflicting moral issues that arise in the context of research on children in a way that indicates and does justice to their complexity while at the same time showing that they are not so complex that they are unamenable to reasoned analysis. I believe there is a happy medium between the instant 'gut response' to moral issues so beloved of a certain type of 'practical' person and the endless fine argument of the pure philosopher that we in the field of applied ethics must constantly seek. While I suspect this present offering tends too far towards endless and not-so-fine argument, I hope that at least it demonstrates that the general framework of principles offered by Beauchamp and Childress can be applied usefully to the moral analysis of the real moral problems that arise in medical research on children in particular and in medical practice in general.

NOTES

1 T. L. Beauchamp and J. F. Childress (1989) *Principles of Biomedical Ethics* (3rd edn), Oxford: Oxford University Press.
2 Hippocratic oath, in British Medical Association (1988) *Philosophy and Practice of Medical Ethics*, London: BMA, pp. 95–6.
3 I. Chalmers and M. Baum (1982) 'Consent to randomised treatment [letter]', *Lancet* ii: 1,051.
4 R. Gillon (1989) 'Medical treatment, medical research and informed consent', *Journal of Medical Ethics* 15: 3–5, 11.
5 M. S. Komrad (1983) 'A defence of medical paternalism: maximising patients' autonomy', *Journal of Medical Ethics* 9: 38–44.
6 C. R. Newton (1976) *General Principles of Law* (3rd edn), London: Sweet & Maxwell, pp. 259–63.

7 G. Williams (1983) *Textbook of Criminal Law* (2nd edn), London: Stevens, pp. 572–6.
8 Mental Health Act 1983, section 3.
9 *Gillick* v. *West Norfolk and Wisbech Area Health Authority* [1986] A.C. 112–207.
10 Reported in the annual report for 1962–3 of the Medical Research Council, Cmnd 2382, pp. 21–5; reprinted in Medical Research Council (1964) 'Responsibility in investigations on human subjects', *British Medical Journal* 2: 178–80.
11 Declaration of Helsinki, in British Medical Association (1988) *Philosophy and Practice of Medical Ethics*, London: BMA, pp. 99–102.
12 R. H. Nicholson (ed.) (1986) *Medical Research with Children: Ethics, Law and Practice*, Report of an Institute of Medical Ethics working party, Oxford: Oxford University Press.
13 M. Smith (1985) 'Taking blood from children causes no more than minimal harm', *Journal of Medical Ethics* 11: 127–31.
14 J. K. Mason and R. A. McCall Smith (1987) *Law and Medical Ethics* (2nd edn), London: Butterworth, p. 271.
15 Nicholson (1986), op. cit., pp. 125–39.
16 P. D. G. Skegg (1984) *Law, Ethics and Medicine*, Oxford: Clarendon Press, pp. 30–117.
17 M. Brazier (1987) *Medicine, Patients and the Law*, Harmondsworth: Pelican, pp. 288–93.
18 I. M. Kennedy and A. Grubb (1989) *Medical Law: Texts and Materials*, London: Butterworth, pp. 846–943.
19 See Colin J. Morley, Chapter 1 in this volume.
20 W. A. Silverman (1985) *Human Experimentation: A Guided Step into the Unknown*, Oxford: Oxford University Press, pp. 173–9.

6

STERILIZATION ABUSE
Women and consent to treatment
Heather Draper

In recent years, the term 'sterilization abuse' has been coined as a description of those instances where the subject's or patient's valid consent was overruled, discounted or impossible due to an incompetence to consent to medical intervention. This chapter centres on sterilization abuse as an act of paternalism: where sterilization is performed or withheld because of some view of the subject's best interests formed by a third party.

This discussion is concerned with contraceptive sterilization – where the intention is the permanent removal of reproductive capacity as a means of family planning. It should be distinguished from eugenic sterilization, where the intention is to prevent reproduction in those who are considered to have undesirable genes, etc., and also from therapeutic sterilization, where the intention is to prevent some harm to the patient. Therapeutic sterilization might be performed to prevent harm resulting from reproduction itself, as in the case of a woman with a heart too weak to cope with pregnancy or labour; or else it is the side-effect of removing diseased reproductive organs, for instance a hysterectomy of a cancerous uterus. Since contraception falls within the realms of family planning, it could be argued that it is different from other medical intervention, being a voluntary procedure which contributes towards personal well-being in a way not normally associated with clinical practice, and related to it only by virtue of the specialized and technical skills required to perform it.[1]

Sterilization is an increasingly popular method of contraception,[2] being quick and easy to perform, intended to be permanent and relatively free of undesirable side-effects, very reliable, and unobtrusive during sexual activity. The ethical issues arise, therefore,

77

not from the nature of the operation itself, but rather from the circumstances in which it is given or withheld; namely, those cases previously defined as sterilization abuse. After assessing the statistics offered as evidence of such abuse, three areas will be examined where paternalism is prevalent; first, the case of those seeking a sterilization because they neither have nor want any children at all; second, the use of sterilization within marriage, where the consent of both partners is a precondition of sterilization; and finally, the sterilization of mentally handicapped women as highlighted in 1987 by rulings of *Re B* and *T* v. *T* and in 1989 by the case of *F*.[3] Some clarification of what constitutes valid consent is also required.

Culver and Gert proposed the formula 'valid consent' as a replacement for 'informed' or 'voluntary' consent,[4] since the latter wrongly suggest that information and freedom from coercion are the necessary and sufficient prerequisites of consent. Valid consent has four elements:

1 A decision (either accepting or declining some intervention).
2 Adequate information, including all relevant clinical, religious, social and cultural details. To be informed requires both an understanding *and* an appreciation or assimilation of the data provided.
3 Freedom from coercion (defined by Culver and Gert as pressure which no reasonable person could resist), which includes any threat implicit or explicit, to withdraw some or all services in the event of non-cooperation but which ought not to restrict any doctor from making a genuine and open attempt to present a personal recommendation. It is worth noting that coercion can be achieved by the manner in which the information is presented, for instance by the order in which it is given or by laying greater and undue emphasis on one set of side-effects.
4 Competence, which has two constituents: first, an understanding of what it means to consent and that such a decision is now being required of one, and second, the ability to understand and appreciate all the data necessary to make an informed decision. When patients are competent in both these respects, their consent is valid irrespective of whether their doctor agrees with their final decision. Conformity to neither criterion is the mark of total incompetence. Culver and Gert made another category, simple consent, to apply to those cases where the subject understands only that some decision is required.

Competence to give simple consent generates ethical problems when the patient offers a decision which conflicts with the assessment of her best interests made by some third party. Culver and Gert conclude that while simple *consent* to some procedure may be overruled,[5] simple *refusal of consent* ought not to be overruled without considerable justification. Their distinction is based upon the belief that it is a greater injustice to impose a treatment that is unwanted than it is to withhold one where the patient has merely acquiesced with their doctor's recommendation.

> We obviously think that just as with competent patients so with those incompetent to give valid consent, it is a much more serious matter to treat without consent ... than not to treat even though simple consent has been given. In the former case, we actively impose something on the patient; in the latter, we simply refuse to do something agreed by the patient. Thus, we give simply refusal of consent ..., by a patient incompetent to give valid refusal of consent, much more weight than simple consent by the same patient. This seems to reverse the traditional practice, whereby a simple consent by such a patient is taken to be valid, and a simple refusal is all too easily overruled.[6]

It is this understanding of valid consent which will form the basis of the following exploration of gaining consent for contraceptive sterilization.

POSSIBLE INDICATIONS OF STERILIZATION ABUSE

Writers in the USA have pointed to certain statistical disparities in the sterilization rate as evidence of the prevalence of sterilization abuse. Sterilization, they argue, is common among those social groups most vulnerable to paternalism: the poor and the uneducated, women and ethnic minorities. Whereas, among white middle and upper classes, vasectomies are more common than tubal ligations, among the lower income and minority groups the opposite trend is seen, a difference which is only exaggerated if hysterectomies are included in the figures. Petchesky, for instance, cites figures suggesting that female sterilizations in 1971 represented only one-fifth of all voluntary sterilizations but that by 1977 this figure had risen to three-fifths.[7] Similarly, the Committee on Abortion Rights and Against Sterilization Abuse argues that among low income groups sterilization occurred at a much younger age (24–34 years) while in the middle and upper classes, the rate began to climb only at the age of 35-plus years.[8] Finally, Ford claimed that in 37 per cent of low income couples aged between 25 and 34 years at least one partner would be sterilized, generally the woman.[9]

Statistics from the UK support some of these claims. For instance, whereas among non-manual workers (white-collar) men are four times more likely to be sterilized than their partners, among manual workers, sterilization is more commonly performed on female partners, at a rate of four to three.[10] Similarly, the sterilization rate among women married to manual workers stood at 29 per cent in 1983 as opposed to 26 per cent among those married to non-manual workers.[11] Overall, however, it is only among the age group 40–44 years that female sterilization is more prevalent than vasectomy.[12] The balance between the sexes seems to have righted itself from seven women to three men in 1970, to six women to five men in 1976, to five to five in 1983.[13] The sterilization rate in the UK has risen sharply: in 1970 only 4 per cent of married women relied on sterilization (of either partner) as a means of contraception; this figure rose to 15 per cent in 1976 and to 24 per cent in 1983.[14] This increase is, however, thought almost entirely due to the increase in those sterilized after the age of 30 years, with no obvious change in the rate among the young, childless or single.[15] However, Wellings does suggest that sterilization is now being considered by couples immediately they decide that their family is large enough, rather than being viewed as a procedure to be undertaken only when the need for reliable contraception becomes urgent. Thus, those who are sterilized under the age of 30 years have at least as many children as those sterilized from the age of 30-plus years.[16]

All statistics are open to interpretation. Any disparities could be explained either in terms of personal preference and taste, or as resulting from some necessity or economic policy. For instance, the increase in the vasectomy rate in the UK from 1970 to 1983 could be cited as evidence of changing social attitudes towards and by women, and of shifts in the notions of contraceptive responsibility. However, it is more likely to be due to the fact that from 1972, vasectomies for contraceptive purposes were included within the NHS by the NHS (Family Planning) Amendment Act. Similarly, as low income groups are more likely to be dependent on the earnings of the female partner, and because such couples often have their children from their late teens onwards, it is not surprising that such women are younger when they consider sterilization than their middle- and upper-class counterparts. However, it is also probably true that the sterilization rate is highest among those groups where termination of pregnancy (TOP) is relatively expensive or unavailable giving the poor an added incentive to seek a sterilization on economic grounds.[17]

What we know without recourse to statistics is that one's education affects the ease with which one is able to give valid consent. Those who start their families early, often do so at the cost of their education. Recent moves to simplify official documents are commendable, but many people still require extra time and help to comprehend the consent forms which they are expected to sign. Some may not be able to read, others cannot read English. Some immigrant groups have an insufficient grasp of verbal English to understand the advice their doctor gives them. It is also thought that patients generally remember only 37–50 per cent of the information imparted in the average consultation.[18] Many patients lack the confidence to raise questions when receiving advice from a physician. Clearly, therefore, some people are going to experience great difficulties with the process of giving their valid consent.

Even if it is granted that the disparities in the sterilization rate only reflect personal preference, and even if we reject the notion of individuals being compelled by social circumstances to have a sterilization which they do not really want, it is still plain that the largest user group, in the USA at least, also requires the most help when making the decision about whether or not to be sterilized. Thus, while these statistics may not be used as proof of sterilization abuse *per se*, it is possible to envisage that doctors, when dealing with the individuals who comprise these more vulnerable groups, may be tempted to make paternalistic decisions on their behalf. To do so is quicker and more convenient than ensuring that valid consent is obtained.

It may also be assumed that if all of those sterilized had given their valid consent to the operation, there would be fewer requests for reversal of voluntary sterilization (RVS), as such requests often represent a failure to gain valid consent. This has been illustrated by many, including Wendy Savage, who claims:

there is abundant evidence that some doctors continue to press their ideas upon women, and do not allow them the right to choose freely if and when to be sterilised.[19]

She supports this allegation by citing some of her own cases from Mile End Hospital. For instance, the case of Mrs JW, who was sterilized at the age of 21 years, after the birth of her first child, because her health visitor and GP considered her to be mentally subnormal and therefore able to cope only with one child. The only evidence of subnormality which Savage could find was that Mrs JW had believed the doctor who told her that the sterilization could be reversed after five years! Accordingly, she had written to Mrs Savage requesting a reversal in order to have a child by her second husband. Unfortunately, after three blasts of diathermy, her Fallopian tubes were beyond repair.[20] Mrs JW did not give valid consent because she was misinformed about the nature of her operation. It may even be argued that she was wrongly deemed incompetent to consent.

Petchesky argues that what makes women particularly vulnerable to an unwanted sterilization is the assumption by some family planning clinics and practitioners that it is women who should be the target of contraceptive advice, that they should take the pill or be fitted with an intra-uterine contraceptive device (IUCD) for several years, followed by a period during which they have all the children they desire, whereupon they should be sterilized.[21] Accordingly, if a woman who has several children seeks a TOP, it is not unlikely that she will be persuaded to have a concurrent sterilization. Yet the highest incidence of regret is to be found among those women who had their sterilization at the time of their TOP, especially when they perceived the sterilization to be a precondition of the termination.[22]

Undoubtedly, most patients freely seek to be sterilized and remain satisfied with their decision. This ought not to preclude attempts to protect others against a sterilization which they will ultimately regret. Such efforts need to be grounded in the preservation of valid consent as a prerequisite for this (and all other) procedures. Savage has illustrated how, in some cases, consent is little more than a protection against litigation for the surgeon. Women seeking RVS have complained that they believed their tubal ligation was readily and easily reversed. Either they failed to comprehend the essentially permanent nature of sterilization or they have been misinformed. Without understanding its permanent nature, any consent to a sterilization is less than valid: likewise, in cases where the patient has no choice but to accept a sterilization, or is coerced into so doing. Valid consent also protects individuals from doctors who feel that promoting patient well-being includes making paternalistic decisions about how many children they are able to afford. Clearly, such judgements are not clinical and ought to be carefully distinguished from those which are. Statements such as 'I think that you should have a sterilization' ought to mean 'A sterilization would best serve the interests of your health' and not 'I believe that people ought not to have more children than they can afford to support without state intervention'. The information required to give valid consent can also be used by a couple in making a decision about which partner it would be best to sterilize (the side-effects for women being greater under normal circumstances than those for men).

CONSENT AND THE CHILDFREE

Within the context of family planning, sterilization is a final and effective contraceptive for those who have all the children they want. There is, however, a growing number of couples, and individuals, who make a conscious decision not to have children. In such cases, sterilization is also the most appropriate contraceptive available. Such requests, however, increase the difficulties of providing universal guidelines on sterilization. On the one hand, couples feel indignant that, having made their decision, they are able to use short-term contraceptives indefinitely, but cannot obtain a sterilization which would have the same effect minus the side-effects and risk of pregnancy. On the other hand, doctors are concerned that the sterilization cannot be reversed if such couples change their minds. They suggest that the decision never to have children is not one that can be made accurately before the age of 30–35, if at all.

Along with other members of society, doctors seem to consider that intentions not to have children are short lived, selfish or indicative of perverse sexual preferences. In short, normal people want children. The attitude that couples should have and want to have children has been labelled 'pronatalism'. Those who do not want children identify this as the basis of the reluctance to give them a sterilization. They insist that they are not childless but childfree, arguing that there are other goals, equally fulfilling for those who choose to pursue them as childrearing is for those who do not. One of their strongest arguments is that the irreversible decision to have children is rarely questioned unlike the irreversible decision not to do so. Veevers completed an extensive study of the childfree and concluded that there are factors which can distinguish those who maintain their desire to remain childfree from those who do not.[23] She also catalogued the extent to which childfree couples are subjected to pronatalistic pressure from peer groups, family and doctors. She cites several cases in which prescriptions for the contraceptive pill were withheld (sometimes on legitimate, though now outdated, concerns for health) but where no reliable alternative was offered, sterilization being dismissed out of hand. She also outlines stories of couples who had great difficulties obtaining a TOP but were still refused a subsequent sterilization. In all cases, the underlying assumption, sometimes made explicit, was that the couple ought now to be considering having a family and ought not therefore to feel dissatisfied by the withdrawal of effective contraceptives. This attitude has markedly graver implications for those women whose health is placed at risk by the continued use of the contraceptive pill. Veevers' research indicates that the distress caused to such couples by the prospect of being forced to become parents, is no less than that experienced by those desperately seeking to have a child using infertility technology, but the latter receive the sympathy of both the medical profession and society.

To refuse to sterilize someone whose consent to the operation is valid, is an unjustified act of paternalism on at least three counts.

First, the refusal is based on some third party's consideration that their perception of what is in the best interests of the subject is actually better than the subject's own. In straightforward cases of incompetence, the consideration of how to act in accordance with best interests generates problems because we all have differing views about such interests, usually based on how we would wish others to treat us in this unfortunate position. Occasionally, we bring into this decision-making process our own insubstantial prejudices perhaps, for instance, against disabled people. Such conflicting views simply mirror the fact that best interests are as different as individuals themselves. In this respect, there is a presumption in favour of freedom, and a tendency to agree with Mill that neither one person, nor any number of persons, is warranted in saying to another human creature of ripe years that he shall not do with his life for his own benefit what he chooses to do with it. He is the person most interested in his own well-being: the interest which any other person, except in cases of strong personal attachment, can have in it, is trifling compared with that he himself has . . . with respect to his own feelings and circumstances, the most ordinary man or woman has means of knowledge considerably surpassing those that can be possessed by anyone else.[24]

Thus, if we grant that the decision whether or not to bear children is one which we are in the best position to make for ourselves, we must conclude that the childfree are similarly placed. Accordingly, to decide that she or he knows their interests better than they do themselves, is for the doctor to act paternalistically towards the childfree as surely as if she or he performed a sterilization against their will or without their knowledge.

Second, refusing the childfree a sterilization has the effect of coercing them into accepting some other mode of contraception, or into becoming parents. Thus, any subsequent consent, to the fitting of an IUCD, for instance, is less than valid for it is not the patient's voluntary and preferred choice of intervention. This is not to say that the surgeon could not refuse to sterilize a patient when to do so would cause immediate and direct harm (though it is difficult to find such a case, except one falling into the wider category of non-urgent operations, the contra-indications to which – because of risks associated with a general anaesthetic or post-operative immobilization – outweigh any possible benefits). Rather the argument has returned to the implementation of valid consent which requires that the patient is informed of all alternative interventions prior to their consent to any one procedure. Culver and Gert illustrate this aspect of valid consent with reference to the management of severe depression for which they claim two possible treatments are available. Electroconvulsive therapy (ECT) takes almost immediate effect, after initial (minor) side-effects such as headaches. Alternatively, the patient can be treated with a course of anti-depressant drugs which also relieve the symptoms but which take much longer to have any effect. For this reason, doctors often recommend ECT.[25] Culver and Gert claim that if the patient is able to give valid consent and chooses the drugs rather than ECT, then this decision must be respected even if, as in the case they cite, the patient's choice is based on a supposedly irrational fear of the alternatives.[26] Thus, even if the doctor considers that the couple are mistaken or irrational in their choice not to have children, their decision to have a sterilization is one which ought to be respected. This does not, however, prevent any doctor from expressing concerns based on his or her experience of other cases. Moreover, to keep silent would be to give them less than adequate information on which to base their consent.

Third, it might be argued that by virtue of their lack of specialized knowledge (that of what it is like to have children) the childfree are actually incompetent to make this *particular* decision for themselves, though competent in most other areas. Such an argument is not valid. First, it is inconsistent to hold that couples with at least one child, and who therefore have proven pronatalistic tendencies, are able to decide that they want no more children, while refusing to accept that couples with no pronatalistic tendencies whatsoever are incompetent to make this same decision. Furthermore, any argument to the contrary calls into question the competence of anyone without children to consent to starting a family. Second, we generally hold that, all other things being equal, we have an equal right of access to medical help as others. This is not an argument about the deployment of scarce resources nor about the distinction between ordinary and extraordinary treatment. Rather, it is about expecting some standardization of care, access to which is not restricted by the irrelevant personal beliefs of the providers of care. While I can be justifiably refused a heart transplant on the grounds that there is nothing wrong with the heart I already possess, I do not expect to be refused access to contraceptives, such as the Pill, sheath, IUCD or even sterilization, when such interventions are provided freely and without cost to others. In the case of the heart transplant, my reasons for wanting a replacement heart will be considerably different to those given by someone whose own heart is failing. However, the reason I give for requiring contraceptives will be much the same whether or not I already have children. Similarly, the reasons given by the childfree for seeking a sterilization are barely distinguishable from those given by parents who have all the children they want: namely a sterilization is reliable, safe, permanent and so on. Thus, it is difficult to see how a paternalistic decision to refuse the operation can be justified. That the childfree operate to a different set of priorities is no reason to deny them equal access to sterilization facilities.

Obviously, clinicians and surgeons are concerned that no one should be sterilized who may later regret this decision. Reversal of voluntary sterilization is not without risks nor can success be guaranteed. One of the aims of those exploring the reasons given by patients requesting reversal of sterilization is to isolate groups of individuals who are statistically likely to regret their decision. Veevers' research suggests that the childfree cannot really be included in this group. However, rather than implementing guidelines and preconditions governing sterilization, such as a lower age limit or existing children, greater progress would be made by ensuring that valid consent to each and every operation is gained. If there are concerns that the childfree or very young are likely to regret their decision (which is by no means certain) then this is information which must be given to patients so that they can decide for themselves whether to proceed with the operation immediately, or to wait for a few more years.

MUTUAL CONSENT IN MARRIAGE

In its ethical guidelines, the British Medical Association (BMA) states:

> the custom of obtaining the consent of the patient's spouse to operations on the reproductive organs is one of courtesy rather than legal necessity. Nevertheless, because the patient's partner may *properly* hold that he or she has an interest in such operations it is good practice to obtain the consent of both partners.[27]

This argument seems to be based on the view that as sexual fidelity makes one dependent upon one's partner to reproduce, anything one's partner does to their reproductive organs affects one's own reproductive capacity. Accordingly, many agree with the BMA that this legitimate interest in one's partner can be translated into mutual consent prior to sterilization. Normally this assumption raises no ethical issues as the decision to seek sterilization is one jointly made and agreed upon by both partners. Problems arise only when one partner refuses to give their consent, or the patient declines to inform their spouse about the proposed operation. Where mutual consent is held to be a precondition of sterilization, the operation must be withheld in those cases where the partner's consent is not forthcoming. Such a consequence is unacceptable.

First, proper interest need not be interpreted in terms of mutual consent. The interest stems from the harm of being denied reproductive opportunities by remaining, in ignorance, sexually faithful to a sterilized partner. Accordingly, proper interest entitles the spouse only to *know* about the operation. Once aware of their partner's sterilization they can exercise their own reproductive freedom by leaving the relationship to have children with someone else. It can therefore be argued that the rights of the spouse extend only to knowledge of the operation, and not to any right of consent.

Second, the BMA's recommendation is unacceptable because the concept of consent is meaningful if, and only if, the subject can freely choose to refuse their consent; in this case, to veto the sterilization. This would mean that proper interest has moved beyond the 'right to consent' into the realms of the 'right to control'. Moreover, the same argument might consistently be employed to give the spouse the right to deny their partner access to an indefinite supply of contraceptives, for as it has already been noted, the constant use of contraception has the same effect as sterilization. Likewise, pushing the argument to its extremes, the spouse could argue that their partner's continued sexual abstinence is also an unacceptable restriction of their reproductive capacity, giving them a justification for rape.[28] A similar argument could also be used to veto a proposed TOP.[29] Clearly, proper interest in one's partner's reproductive organs ought not to extend indirectly into control over their use, and for this reason it ought to be interpreted only as the partner's right to know about the sterilization. It is futile to argue that the spouse has the right to retain their reproductive freedom by modifying that of their partner.[30]

This leaves the question of the doctor's obligation in those cases where the patient refuses to inform their spouse of an intended sterilization. As it is clear that their spouse need not consent to the operation, the doctor's dilemma is not so much whether or not to perform the operation, but whether or not to inform the spouse on the basis of their right to know and, obviously, to do so without the consent of their patient.

Few doubt that confidentiality is one of the corner-stones of effective medical care. Without it a patient's medical history would be almost worthless since a doctor could never be sure that the patient was telling the whole truth as the patient would certainly filter out information which she or he was unwilling to have published abroad. Thus, contentions centred on confidentiality are concerned with determining whether it is an absolute prescription or whether it is of only relative value (that it rests on balancing the possible harms of disclosure against the possible harm – usually to others – of maintaining silence).

In response to such concerns, the General Medical Council (GMC) detailed eight circumstances under which confidentiality may be broken:

1 The patient or his legal adviser gives written consent.
2 Information is shared with other doctors, nurses or health professionals participating in caring for the patient.
3 Where, on medical grounds, it is undesirable to seek the patient's consent, information may sometimes be given in confidence to a close relative.
4 When in the doctor's opinion disclosure of information to some third party other than a relative would be in the best interests of the patient, the doctor must make every effort to get the patient's consent. Only in exceptional circumstances may the doctor go ahead and impart that information without the patient's consent.
5 Information may be disclosed to comply with a statutory requirement, for example notification of an infectious disease.
6 Information may be disclosed where it is so ordered by a court.
7 Rarely, disclosure may be justified on the grounds of public interest which, in certain circumstances such as, for instance, investigation by the police of a grave and serious crime, might override the doctor's duty to maintain his patient's confidence.
8 Information may be disclosed, if necessary, for the purpose of a medical research project approved by some recognized ethical committee.[31]

It can be argued that this list is so open to interpretation (for instance over what is meant by the patient's or public's best interest) that practically any disclosure may be condoned with reference to it. While recognizing this possibility, it should be borne in mind that such disclosures are rightly placed within the content of a strict ethical obligation to maintain confidence.

The only two exceptions which may furnish a doctor with an excuse to inform the spouse, in the context of sterilization, are (4) and (7): disclosures in the interests of the patient and the public (the spouse being a member of the public). The argument from the patient's interests is extremely weak (not least of all because this disclosure is being considered in the light of the best interests of the spouse). Such an argument would require the doctor to make a case such as the one that the patient's intentions may jeopardize his or her marriage and that this is not in his or her best interests. However, providing that the patient has some idea of what she or he is risking, it is surely their personal decision to determine whether such a risk is outweighed by the perceived benefits of a (secret) sterilization. The argument from the spouse's best interests (via the public interest) is only marginally stronger. The case falls on the impossibility of making an argument that the harm to the spouse is sufficiently grave to warrant a breach of confidentiality and all the subsequent harm of so doing (not least of which is a breach of the patient's trust). The harm to the spouse is neither actual or direct; she or he will not become literally infertile as a result of the operation, rather it is the relationship which is affected. Obviously the consequences may be identical where the spouse never discovers that their partner has intentionally rendered themselves infertile. However, it is not unreasonable to suppose that such a spouse, if genuinely concerned to have a(nother) child, would actually begin to investigate why pregnancy has not occurred and would probably thereby discover the truth (after first involving the doctor in another difficult situation of having to tell the truth while simultaneously maintaining confidentiality).

Breach of confidentiality in these circumstances is paternalistic. It is acting against the patient's valid consent, in an apparent attempt to moderate the patient's moral behaviour. Viewing such an action as paternalism actually serves to clarify the issue. In seemingly forcing the patient to accept his or her responsibilities, the doctor is actually acknowledging that the responsibility for informing the spouse does indeed rest with the patient. Once this is recognized, it is apparent that the doctor's ethical obligations are fulfilled once she or he has told the patient of their partner's legitimate interest in the operation. Once this is done, the onus is upon the patient to inform his or her spouse. This is a moral duty and he or she is the only party who can be held morally responsible for any harm to the spouse by a failure to do so. Moreover, by insisting on disclosure, the doctor may compel the patient to withdraw their request which, once again, has the effect of curtailing their reproductive freedom in order to protect that of their spouse.

Very clearly, the BMA is correct to assert that the most desirable situation is one where both parties agree to the operation and this undoubtedly occurs in the majority of cases. Likewise, the physician or surgeon should aim to obtain the assent of both. The purpose of this discussion is merely to reiterate that ultimately only the patient's valid consent is required for any operation, and the doctor is under no ethical imperative to make the spouse's consent, or even knowledge, a prerequisite for sterilization.

THE STERILIZATION OF MENTALLY DISABLED PEOPLE

The sterilization of mentally disabled people raises issues in consent where those concerned are deemed unable to consent for themselves and a third party is appointed to give proxy consent. In three such cases, this third party was the court. In April 1987 the House of Lords determined that Jeanette, a 17-year-old woman with an intellectual age of between 2 and 6 years, could be given a sterilization as the most appropriate means of serving her best interests. The court heard that Jeanette had no understanding of the relationship between sex and contraception, would be unable to cope with the pain and the psychological trauma of pregnancy and confinement and would certainly never be capable of rearing a child herself or consenting to marriage. She did, however, have the normal sex drive and inclinations for a woman of her years; she had made sexual advances to members of staff at the hostel where she stayed and had shown sexual interest in other male residents. Expert opinion was that a regime of contraceptive drugs could not be established due to aggressive and uncooperative outbursts. Also, it was believed that contraceptive drugs might have undesirable side-effects including further weight gain and exacerbated epilepsy. Accordingly, if Jeanette were to be permitted the benefits of sexual relationships without the 'unmitigated disaster' of pregnancy,[32] a sterilization must be performed. In July 1987 a similar case, T v. T, was heard before WOOD J. In this case the woman concerned was 19 and pregnant. Like Jeanette, she was severely mentally disabled and epileptic. Unlike Jeanette she was over the age under which it is possible for the court, using wardship, to consent on her behalf, either to a termination or to a sterilization, both of which were held to be in her best interests on similar ground to those given in the Jeanette case. WOOD J. held that it would be unjust for T to be denied 'the benefit of surgical treatment' simply because she was unable to consent for herself.[33] He accordingly declared that in the circumstances a termination and concurrent sterilization would not be unlawful. The difficulty of providing treatment for incompetent patients over the age of majority was also raised in 1989 when ultimately the House of Lords held that it was lawful to sterilize a 35-year-old woman referred to as F, who was also mentally disabled and actively engaged in a sexual relationship with a fellow resident of the institution where she lived.

In 1975 a court in Sheffield had blocked the proposed sterilization of a mentally disabled girl known as D. Between 1975 and 1987 the sterilization of mentally disabled people had been of sporadic interest in the academic journals. Lucy Crain, arguing against such sterilizations, cited two anecdotal cases which she felt highlighted the dangers of permitting these sterilizations to proceed.[34] The first was of a mildly disabled man, sterilized at the age of 12 while in the care of an institution. His sterilization came to Crain's notice when, at the age of 22, having a car, a job and a fiancée with whom he hoped to found a family, he made enquiries about having his sterilization reversed. The second case was of an aphasic woman whose hysterectomy was performed at the request of her mother, to save her from the 'messy bother of menstruation'.[35] Two years later, her mother discovered her stealing sanitary towels and smearing them with a red solution to mimic menstrual bleeding so that she could be like her workmates. She was 19 years old. In a further case, provided for this chapter by Gavin Fairbairn, a physician recommended a sterilization for 'Jackie' as a method of curbing her distasteful habit of eating her used sanitary pads. Jackie ate constantly anything which came to hand including, at times, her own excreta.

Clearly, these latter cases present ethical problems. The sterilizations of Jackie and the aphasic woman were not proposed out of any sense of what was in their best interests as both were exposed to the risk of major abdominal surgery to satisfy the tastes of others for what is acceptable or decent behaviour. Similarly, in Crain's first case, which not only raises the question of whether it is possible accurately to predict the extent of mental disability in children, but also more gravely, whether mentally disabled males ought ever to be sterilized. For even if this man had been severely mentally disabled, it is difficult to see how such an operation could ever serve his best interests as he could never become pregnant in any circumstances. Thus, in each case, it seems that it was thought fit to perform a procedure upon mentally disabled people, which would have been unacceptable for the mentally able but incompetent (children, for instance). The operations were unacceptable because they were not apparently intended solely to improve the quality of life of the subject despite the principle that only the best interests of the subject of any procedure should be taken into account when giving proxy consent.

The cases of Jeanette and T are not so obviously problematic for, prima facie at least, the best interests of the women do seem to have been highly regarded.[36] The major differences between the two cases are that of T's pregnancy and her age (over 18). For the purposes of this chapter, the pregnancy is largely irrelevant being important here only in so far as it was used to initiate the discussions about sterilization. It would be inappropriate here to discuss the status of the foetus, its right to life or the ethics of the termination (though some of what follows may be relevant to such a discussion). In both the case of T and of F, the judges noted that it is tragic for a patient to be denied treatment merely because she or he is unfortunate enough not to be able to consent to it. This legal situation has meant that, strictly speaking, only life-saving procedures can be performed for such individuals and has led to untold suffering as minor ailments, such as tooth decay, are left untreated. It has been argued already, that it is not the age of the subject which makes the difference when it comes to consent, but rather their competence. It is not therefore inconsistent to argue here that the law preventing proxy consent in the case of adults does need to be changed, providing, as always, the best interests of the subject concerned remain the paramount and sole concern of any person or body giving proxy consent on their behalf.

The arguments about the cases of Jeanette and T seem to fall into two camps. First, it can be argued that best interests vary from person to person. The interests of mentally disabled people will not, therefore, be quite the same as those of the mentally able population so that while it would not be ethical under ordinary circumstances to perform a contraceptive sterilization on a child or unconscious patient, it may be ethical to sterilize a person who is mentally disabled. After all, a decision against sterilization and favouring the long-term use of contraception backed up with terminations of pregnancy, effectively curtails the reproductive capacity but also exposes the subject to the side-effects of contraceptives such as the pill and, more seriously, to the problems of repeated terminations (one of which is, ironically, sterility). Furthermore, it can be argued that mental disability is a largely irreversible form of incompetence. Unlike children, severely mentally disabled people will not mature to a state where they are able to make decisions for themselves. Thus, the side-effects of long-term use of contraception and termination of pregnancy cannot be off-set against the good of allowing individuals to make important decisions for themselves. Second, it can be argued that to sterilize mentally disabled people is to fail to respect them as individuals. At its weakest presentation this argument resorts to rhetoric, arguing that we tend to view the sterilization of mentally disabled people in the same light as we view the sterilization of our pet cat. However, stronger versions seek to show the ways in which sterilization involves using mentally disabled people as means to some other end.

The relationship between carer and cared for is a very intimate one, and to some extent it is fair to say that making the carer's job easier will also improve the quality of care received by the cared for, such that things which prima facie appear to be in the interests of the carer are in fact also in the interest of the cared for. Thus, in the case of Jackie, it might be argued that since the eating of her sanitary towels seems to have been the last straw for her otherwise patient and sincere mother, Jackie's interests were best served by removing this apparent obstacle to her remaining under the care, at home, of her mother, rather than by insisting that she was being used as a means to an end which would have resulted in her being placed in an institution, divorced from her loving family and their quality of care. However, it is difficult to see how far arguments of this kind ought to extend. An alternative solution to Jackie's problem would have been to wire her teeth up. This would have prevented all her antisocial behaviour at a stroke! It would also have improved the quality of care given to Jackie by her family, who would have had additional resources to spend on her as a result of not having continually to replace the household items she routinely ate. This, at the cost of Jackie being deprived of the comfort she gained by feeling that her mouth was full; however, both these solutions are more radical than the solution found by Jackie's social workers. They blocked the sterilization by making her a ward of court and placed her in an institution full-time. Here her habit of eating her sanitary towels was subjected to negative reinforcement and substitute food was provided. After six months, she was returned to her mother's care and only very occasionally ate her sanitary towels thereafter.

Jackie's case illustrates quite clearly how last resorts have a habit of becoming first options, obscuring other means of tackling problems because they are quick and, apparently, easy. Arguments favouring the sterilization of mentally disabled people abound with examples of where the sterilization is viewed as a means to an end which will, it is claimed, result in better conditions for the subjects of it.

The most popular of these is that sterilization enables mentally disabled people to engage in sexual relationship without the undesirable side-effects of pregnancy. Such relationships are as beneficial to mentally disabled people as others, it is claimed; they certainly fit into the current ideology of 'normalization' programmes. Such claims put the opponents of sterilization in the position of appearing to be denying to mentally disabled people something which they themselves treasure. The argument, however, needs more careful examination.

First, a sterilization does not ensure sexual freedom. For this privacy, education and mixed sex establishments are required, run by liberal-minded workers who do not find the prospect of sexual relationships between their clients utterly distasteful. There is little point sterilizing an individual who will spend her life in segregated incarceration or under inflexible supervision. Second, it would be wrong to argue that all sexual relationships are beneficial; exploitative ones certainly are not. Several factors need to be considered here. Sterilization offers protection against pregnancy, not sexual abuse. Indeed, it may even encourage sexual abuse since the perpetrator will be certain that his crimes will not be uncovered by an unexplained pregnancy. Sterilization cannot be a substitute for adequate care and protection of those who are unable to defend their own rights. Moreover, granted that the proposed subjects of these sterilizations are incompetent, it is possible to question the status of any consent which they give to sexual activity. This is not to argue that sexual activity ought not to be allowed, but rather that it needs to be monitored. We might use here the model of our reaction to the sexual activity of children. The consent of a child to sexual activity with an adult is never an acceptable justification for such activity. At the same time, we accept (or at least ignore) the games that children play with each other as a form of sexual exploration, provided of course that both children want to play. Accordingly, while we need to accept the relationships formed among mentally disabled individuals, we ought to feel at least as outraged by instances of exploitation imposed by so-called normal persons upon mentally disabled people, as we do those imposed upon children. The former can only be further obscured by a sterilization. Once again, sterilization is no substitute for adequate care. Nor should sterilization be viewed as the safety net for inadequate care. It is too great a price to pay and too likely to encourage complacency.

There is one further set of arguments which need to be discussed, and these concern views about the pregnancy itself and the subsequent child. One of the things which seems to have been taken for granted in Jeanette's case was that pregnancy would be 'an unmitigated disaster'.[37] It was asserted that Jeanette would not be able to understand the changes and pain of pregnancy and labour, that she might find the ordeal alarming and if a Caesarean section were given to circumvent the labour, she would be likely to rip at the healing wound. The Lords were probably correct to assume that childbearing would bring Jeanette little pleasure. However, the gravity of the decision being made warranted more than presumption that significant mental and physical harm would result, yet no supporting documentary evidence was cited.[38] Nor was it shown that one needed to understand the changes and pain in order to cope with them. Similarly, it was claimed that both Jeanette and *T* disliked small children and treated their dolls badly. There undoubtedly exist many successful mothers who felt the same at the age of 17 or 19. Also, it would have to be shown that Jeanette treated her dolls as though they were children, or indeed that any child does. Finally, there is the question of the effect it would have on a child to be born to mentally disabled parents. Here we are faced with a clash of interests in that concerns for the fate of the child seem to weigh against the possible interests of mentally disabled people not to be the subject of sterilization or termination of pregnancy. This seems to present the gravest problems for those persons whose mental disability is such that they will be loving but largely inadequate or unintentionally neglectful parents, possibly unable to provide their child with an atmosphere of stimulation sufficient to allow an intellectual development greater than their own. However, the child is additionally handicapped by this society's reluctance to provide his or her parents with the help which they would need to ensure that his or her welfare was protected. Having stated this, it also seems to be unjust that the welfare of the child is an issue with mentally disabled people but not with other members of society whose attitude towards their children is also undesirable. If the best interests of subsequent children is a sufficient criterion upon which to perform a sterilization then this ought to be the case regardless of the potential parent's IQ. It also raises the whole issue of whether it is ever appropriate to make proxy decisions for the incompetent based on what is best for others rather than, or in addition to, themselves. Granted that any subsequent child could be adopted, one must also bear in mind whether adoption really is worse than no life at all. This being the case, there seem to be good grounds for ensuring that no children are born whose parents are likely to give them up for adoption.

Taking all these arguments into account, it seems that the issue does indeed rest on consent and how this is to be given on behalf of those unable to consent for themselves. Here, the rule that only the interests of the subject ought to be taken into account functions well. It ensures that each case is judged on its own merits without reference to other cases. It also means that each mentally disabled person is seen as an end in themselves and not a means to some other end. However, this aim is also flouted when we refuse to accept that any case of sterilization is ever justified, on the ground that such cases reflect a general disregard for the mentally disabled as persons. For in this case, the person concerned is being used as a means to the end of protecting the welfare of this vulnerable group as a whole.

CONCLUSION

This discussion has highlighted some groups of people particularly vulnerable to sterilization abuse. It has been shown how strict adherence to valid consent offers some protection to those who are actually competent to consent for themselves. In this respect, the notion of valid consent offers a far greater defence than a series of guidelines, including such items as a minimum age limit for sterilization or an arbitrary number of children. It is important for all overseeing the consent process to recognize that marriage and the absence of children do not constitute another variety of incompetence to consent. Certainly counselling prior to sterilization helps to ensure that valid consent is forthcoming, by stressing the permanent nature of the operation, discussing other contraceptive alternatives (including the sterilization of the other partner) and determining that all concerned understand exactly what it is they are committing themselves to. All consent forms, not merely those for sterilization, need to be written in the patient's native language, in a simple and non-technical style which makes the irreversible and contraceptive nature of the operation clear, spelling out the alternatives and inherent risks. This statement ought to be read aloud as a matter of course, the onus not being placed on an illiterate patient to ask for this service. No conditions should ever be attached to a sterilization, for instance the withdrawal of other services or a termination of pregnancy.

It is possible that, in the future, use of sterilization and infertility technology such as *in vitro* fertilization using frozen sperm and ovum, may be combined by individuals wishing for both reliable contraception and the possibility of children in the future. This being the case, many of the fears that doctors have about offering sterilizations to those without children may be allayed. Such a combination of available technology will of course be dependent on the medical profession's willingness to release their stranglehold of paternalism on such procedures, and the government's willingness to finance this innovation.

The sterilization of mentally disabled people remains a difficult ethical area, walking a tight rope between using the disabled individual as a means to the end of promoting the rights of this group as a whole, and consideration for their carers and subsequent offspring. Since it is clearly unfair to make irreversible decisions by proxy at an age where all the necessary information (future progress and desires, etc.) is not available, there should be a halt called on all contraceptive sterilizations of mentally disabled minors. In order not to exclude sterilization as a possibility for the future, it is therefore necessary for a review of the law concerning wardship in those cases where it is unlikely that competence will ever be attained. Similarly, research into the attitudes of mentally disabled women towards pregnancy, labour and children is required to avoid court decisions being grounded on assumptions with respect to these attitudes. Where such sterilizations are considered they must be solely in the interests of the individual concerned. For this reason, it seems unlikely that it will ever be necessary to sterilize a mentally disabled man. Furthermore, the sterilization ought to be realistically necessary in terms of existing or foreseeable sexual activity.

The case involving Jeanette was rapidly followed by that of T and F, and there is obviously an urgent need for these matters to be resolved before such cases form a legal precedent which permits the more arbitrary and less considered sterilization of mentally disabled people.

NOTES

1 The view that those seeking contraceptive services are not ill by normal definition, and therefore constitute a special category of patient, is expanded more fully in H. J. A. Draper (1986) PhD thesis, 'A Philosophical and Ethical Appraisal of Clinical Intervention in, and Control over, Contraception and Reproduction', University of Manchester.

2 K. Wellings (1986) 'Trends in contraceptive method usage since 1970', *British Journal of Family Planning* 12: 17.

3 *Re B (A Minor) (Wardship: Sterilisation)* [1987] 2 All E.R. 206 H.L.; *T v. T* [1988] 1 All E.R. 613; *F v. West Berkshire Health Authority* [1989] 2 All E.R. 545 H.L.

4 C. M. Culver and B. Gert (1982) *Philosophy in Medicine*, Oxford: Oxford University Press.

5 For instance, by their own doctor, another doctor called to give a second opinion, their guardian or even a court of law.

6 Culver and Gert (1982), op. cit., p. 61.

7 R. Petchesky (1970) 'Reproduction, ethics and public policy', *Hastings Centre Report* 9(5): 30.

8 Committee for Abortion Rights and Against Sterilisation Abuse (CARASA) (1979) *Women Under Attack*, New York: CARASA, p. 30.

9 K. Ford (1978) 'Contraceptive use in the United States 1973–1976', *Family Planning Perspectives* 1(5): 268.

10 Wellings (1986), op. cit., p. 20.

11 ibid., p. 20.

12 ibid., p. 20.

13 ibid., pp. 19–20.

14 ibid., p. 17.

15 ibid., p. 18.

16 ibid., p. 19.

17 Petchesky (1979), op. cit., pp. 30–1.

18 P. Ley (1976) 'Toward better doctor–patient communication', in A. E. Bennett (ed.) *Communication between Doctors and Patients*, Nuffield Provisional Hospitals Trust, p. 85. This figure varies according to the number of statements presented to the patient. Two pieces of information can usually be accurately recalled, whereas, if eight or more pieces are given only half will be remembered. Outpatients recall even less of the information given to them during their consultation (37.2–54 per cent) than do those patients consulting with their GPs (50 per cent).

19 W. Savage (1982) 'Taking liberties with women: abortion, sterilisation and contraception', *International Journal of the Health Services* 12(2): 294.

20 ibid., pp. 293–4.

21 R. Petchesky (1984) *Abortion and Women's Choice*, New York: Longman, p. 178.

22 K. Schywart and A. Kutner (1973) 'A reanalysis of female reaction to sterilisation', *Journal of Nervous Diseases* 156: 354–70. Also H. M. Vemer, P. Colla and D. C. Schoot (1986) 'Women regretting their sterilisation', *Fertility and Sterility* 46(1): 725, who recommend that women ought not to be offered concurrent sterilization along with other gynaecological procedures, even though to do so lessens the risks from anaesthetics compared with two operations. C. E. Lennox, J. A. Mills and G. B. James (1987) 'Reversal of female sterilisation: a comparative study', *Contraception* 35(1): 25, recommend that sterilization is not performed with either TOP or delivery. Many sources cite W. Savage 'Abortion and sterilization: should the operations be combined?' (1981) in *British Journal of Family Planning* 7: 8–12, and J. M. Emens and J. E. Olive, 'Timing of female sterilisation', in *BMJ* 3: 1,126, who make similar recommendations and give some indication of the extent of these practices in previous years.

23 J. E. Veevers (1980) *Childless by Choice*, Toronto: Butterworth.

24 J. S. Mill *On Liberty*, Harmondsworth: Pelican, pp. 142–3.

25 Culver and Gert (1982) op. cit., p. 47.

26 ibid., p. 154–5.

27 British Medical Association (1988) *Philosophy and Practice of Medical Ethics*, London: BMA (my emphasis), p. 33.

28 It is disturbing to note that until recently marital intercourse could never amount to rape in the UK. Recent judgments rectifying this situation are most welcome, even if overdue.

29 In 1978, a husband attempted to prevent his wife's TOP and the case went to court (*Paton* v. *British Pregnancy Advisory Service*). Both the judge and subsequently the European Court of Human Rights found that he had no right so to do and that his right to family life was subordinate to the health of the mother. The latter part of the judgment ambiguously suggests that if the mother's health had not been so endangered the father's rights may have been stronger (cf M. Brazier (1987) *Medicine, Patients and the Law*, Harmondsworth: Pelican, pp. 208–9).

30 Note here that until March 1976, a husband's consent was required prior to his wife being fitted with an IUCD.

31 Cited in M. Brazier (1987) *Medicine, Patients and the Law*, Harmondsworth: Pelican, p. 36.

32 *Re B (A Minor) (Wardship: Sterilization)* [1987] 2 AU E.R. 206 at p. 214 *per* Lord Bridge.

33 [1988] 1 AU E.R. 613 at p. 621.

34 L. Crain (1980) 'Sterilisation and the retarded female', *Paediatrics* 66(44): 650–1.

35 ibid., p. 650.

36 At the time of writing there was insufficient evidence available about 'F' to comment in detail.

37 [1987] 2 AU E.R. 206 at p. 214.

38 Or recorded as having been cited in court in the account in *All England Law Reports* as above in Notes 32 and 33.

7

DEPENDENCY REVISITED
The limits of autonomy in medical ethics

Alastair Campbell

A major preoccupation of the 'new' medical ethics (that approach which distances itself from an uncritical acceptance of the code morality of the medical profession itself) has been to establish the centrality of the value of autonomy. One might almost say that 'autonomy' (or more precisely, 'respect for the autonomy of patients') has become a shibboleth by which the true followers of the new ethic identify themselves. I gladly include myself in the group. But I also want to ask myself, has such an emphasis on the centrality of autonomy obscured some other equally important moral values, which modern medicine must also respect? I find myself provoked into asking this question by the political climate of our times, by the uneasy feeling that the philosophers who have defended autonomy are now finding themselves the (mostly unwitting) allies of politicians who are promoting self-reliance as a central moral value. For, if 'autonomy' is to carry a high value, then what is its polar opposite which is to be equivalently disvalued? *Philosophers* would reply 'heteronomy', but popular thought sees it otherwise. Confusing autonomy with independence, the current political mood regards *dependency* as moral inadequacy. The weak and the needy are increasingly being seen as an inconvenient burden which the strong and successful must only grudgingly bear. In medicine the creeping transition from a National Health Service to a mixed system with extra benefits for the more successful seems an obvious outcome of this philosophy of heroic self-reliance. Dependency, especially chronic dependency, becomes a state to be avoided if at all possible.

With these concerns in mind, I shall first ask some questions about the formulation of and the justification for the principle of respect

101

for autonomy. Then I shall suggest some other value assumptions which, while not necessarily rejecting autonomy, cast some doubts on claims about its central position as *the* moral value. Thereafter I shall look at some examples of dependency and at their implications for medical ethics. Finally I shall return to my reservations about the character of the 'new' medical ethics.

DEFINITIONS AND JUSTIFICATIONS

In *Philosophical Medical Ethics*, Raanan Gillon defines autonomy as

the capacity to think, decide, and act (on the basis of such thought and decision) freely and independently.[1]

Gillon goes on to observe that 'The concept of autonomy incorporates the exercise of what Aristotle calls man's specific attribute, rationality.' He describes three aspects of autonomy – of thought, of will and of action – and then elaborates the moral principle of *respect for autonomy* which is designed to safeguard these three types of autonomy in all persons, subject only to the proviso that limits on any individual's autonomy must be imposed when it impinges upon the autonomy of others.

Gillon goes on to point out that, classically, two kinds of justification for the principle of respect for autonomy have been offered: the Kantian argument that the nature of rational beings themselves and of the moral law which their reason discerns *requires* that the autonomy of all be respected; and the Utilitarian argument of Mill, which writes in as an essential component of the general good the liberty of the individual subject. (Gillon himself does not arbitrate between these very different types of justification.)

Finally in some later chapters of Gillon's book, we find familiar arguments about first, the poorly founded claims of medical paternalism to 'know what is best' for the patient, especially when this entails withholding information or failing to obtain consent, and second, the problem of the principle of respect for autonomy when the competence of the patient is under question. In this latter area, Gillon accepts that impairment of will or impairment of reason do provide some justification for making decisions on the patient's behalf, but he warns against using a stricter criterion for the competency of a patient to make medical decisions than we do, for example, in permitting a person to vote or to make other decisions about his or her personal life. Thus, accepting that autonomy is always going to be present or absent to greater or lesser degrees, Gillon argues (in effect) for a prima facie assumption in its favour. It is up to the defender of paternalistic decision-making to justify the overriding of individual autonomy.

Gillon's account may be supplemented by reference to recent similar expositions by Lindley[2] and by Harris.[3] Harris offers the following description of autonomy:

> critical self-determination in which the agent strives to make decisions which are as little marred by defects in reason, information or control as she can make them.[4]

The negative aspects of Harris's account are very usefully elaborated by Richard Lindley. Observing that heteronomy, like (say) baldness, is rarely an absolute state, but more a matter of degree, Lindley suggests that we judge a person's degree of autonomy/heteronomy on both cognitive and conative criteria. A person is *cognitively* heteronomous, either if she holds a set of beliefs which are false, or if the beliefs are held without the active exercise of theoretical reason to establish their truthfulness. A person is *conatively* heteronomous if her actions are determined by desires which she regards as of lesser importance or if she fails to act on what she believes to be her preferred choices ('weakness of the will').[5]

I really have no quarrel with all that has been said in these philosophical expositions. (Indeed they reiterate central points of ethical theory to which many philosophers would subscribe.) My hesitation is rather with what is *not* said by the way of qualification of the principle of respect for autonomy. In particular I consider that the issue of *degrees* of autonomy is insufficiently discussed with a view to its moral significance and that an undue stress on rationality carries attendant dangers of intellectual arrogance. I would therefore like to state quite briefly and dogmatically three main reservations and then in the next section make my own value assumptions more explicit.

1 A converse of saying that autonomy is always a matter of degree (that is there is no time T when individual X is wholly autonomous) is that in *every* situation the individual will have *some* dependence on others. Therefore autonomy should not be discussed in abstraction from dependency.
2 Kant's emphasis on autonomy depends upon his insistence on the distinction between the noumenal and the phenomenal worlds.

Such a radical distinction casts doubt upon the need to respect the autonomy of those whose rationality is impaired, especially if it is permanently impaired. (I believe that this has had serious consequences for many recent philosophical discussions of values in neonatal medicine in particular.)

3 If we attempt, as Mill does, to provide a justification on Utilitarian grounds for the principle of autonomy, the argument is always vulnerable to other claims about what constitutes the good of society. In particular, we can ask whether an emphasis on individual liberty, even when defined in Kantian fashion as autonomy of the will, can of itself necessarily ensure a just and compassionate society.

SOME ALTERNATIVE ASSUMPTIONS ABOUT VALUE

Let me begin this section with some quotations from a stimulating essay referred to in Raanan Gillon's exposition of autonomy, 'Who is autonomous man?', by John Benson.[6] Benson remarks that he doubts if autonomous man (as depicted in recent philosophical discussion) would be very nice to know! As Benson observes, we need to do something to change the 'Faustian cast' of the portrait:

> The ideas of self-creation and of persistent radical self-questioning go together in the picture of the autonomous man as captain of his soul. This needs not obliteration but some re-painting to make the lineaments more homely.[7]

The altered picture which Benson offers us seeks to correct an overemphasis on reason and on a rather arrogant self-sufficiency by suggesting that one may acknowledge the *emotional* components of moral judgments without making morality merely a matter of feeling; and that one can be someone 'whose mind and will have come to embody beliefs and standards which belong to his tradition',[8] without being merely over-compliant or heteronomous in character.

I wish to build on these creative suggestions of Benson by placing the principle of respect for autonomy within another set of values, derived in part from theology. In *Moderated Love* I have attempted to grapple with several moral issues implicit in professional care.[9] One of these is the claim to authority which the professional makes when offering services to the patient or client. In what sense, if any, can we say that the professional 'knows best'? With respect to the medical profession particularly, I believe that this is related to the extent that medicine can mediate *wisdom*, not merely technical knowledge, regarding the human body in its physical and developmental aspects. Such an approach to 'knowing what is best' calls upon the theological doctrine of creation, the idea that in our human nature we can discern (though dimly) what is requisite for our flourishing, our well-being, as creatures of a loving creator. It is at this point that I part company from the Kantian emphasis on rationality and individual autonomy, since I regard the fundamental feature of our creatureliness to be *connectedness*. Here is how I develop this idea in *Moderated Love*:

> To be a creature is to be born of others, to know ourselves through them, to depend upon them and create dependency, to know the pain of losing them and finally to be the instance of that pain to others.[10]

It follows that the autonomous individual is a mere philosopher's abstraction, as unreal as Kant's attempt to separate the phenomenal world from the noumenal world. The need to respond to and be responded to by others never leaves us. It is never a matter of whether to choose to experience dependency, since for most of us dependency is the main feature of our lives. It is rather a question of deciding when demands made *by* us or *upon* us for dependent relationships are inappropriate and unjustified and of discovering how we are to hold in balance the autonomy of ourselves and of others with the necessary dependencies which connect us. Thus a stress on autonomy is (let me suggest rather tendentiously) the *minor* key in medical ethics – the major key should be to discover how to foster appropriate and nurturing dependency.

It may be countered that I need not polarize the issue in this dramatic manner. In the ideal situation *appropriate* dependency is merely the precursor to a restoration of autonomy. After a severe illness or accident I am nurtured back to independence by the appropriate paternalism of the professional staff.[11] The point remains, however, that the beneficent approach of traditional medical ethics can easily be seen as merely temporary, merely instrumental for autonomy, but of no enduring worth in itself. As a result, the chronically dependent became a special problem, an embarrassment to the dominant moral value. Fragility and vulnerability, rather than being seen as appropriate parts of life from the cradle to the grave, became obstacles to be overcome by the self-sufficient man or woman. The *successful* patient is always the one who transcends the state of patienthood. Such a philosophy feeds on many modern myths about illness and about the power of medical science, and eventually it leads to childish illusions about human capabilities and human survival.

At the risk of unduly labouring this point, let me now take a quotation from another theological source – Stanley Hauerwas's recently published collection of essays, *Suffering Presence*.[12] Hauerwas repeatedly claims that medicine is itself a moral endeavour, not simply the exercise of techniques; he believes that the practice of medicine raises in critical form the issue of the moral quality of our community life. Here is how he puts it in a section of the Introduction to the volume entitled 'The Rise (and Fall) of Medical Ethics':

> Medicine involves the needs and interests that we all share. All of us wish to avoid untimely death. All wish to avoid unnecessary suffering. All wish to be cared for when we are hurt. . . . Medicine provides a powerful reminder . . . of our 'nature' as bodily beings beset by illness and destined for death. Yet medicine also reminds us it is our 'nature' to be a community that refuses to let suffering alienate us from one another. The crucial question is what kind of community we should be to be capable of that task.[13]

I shall return to Hauerwas's 'crucial question' in the next section of this chapter, but first I take as a third illustration of alternative value contexts, the descriptions of the medical relationship in William F. May's *The Physician's Covenant: Images of the Healer in Medical Ethics*.[14] May reviews different images of the physician as healer and as teacher. He favours retaining this range in order to avoid the distortions and moral inadequacies of any one of them when it becomes normative. But encompassing them all, he suggests, there is the 'physician's covenant', which he believes most accurately conveys the 'reciprocity of giving and receiving which nourishes the professional relationship'.[15] In 'covenant' we find enshrined that essential element of communal responsibility and interdependence which is essential for the practice of a truly humane medicine. May argues that the contractual ethic (the one implied by the emphasis on liberty or autonomy which I have been questioning) will ultimately fail because it fails to demand from the well and powerful any genuine commitment to the welfare of the ill and the weak. But a covenantal ethic, based ultimately on religious belief in a loving creator, sets the required context for a medical practice committed to protect, nourish and heal the needy, while acknowledging the failures and human vulnerability of those who make such a commitment. In brief, May believes that respect for autonomy is not in itself a sufficiently powerful and comprehensive moral principle to provide an ethical assessment of medical practice.

What then are we to say, in a positive moral sense, of dependency? Let us define it as 'being in relationship to others in a manner which makes them necessary for the fulfilment of some or all of our needs'. The newborn infant provides an example of such dependency: without warmth and nourishment provided by others the child will quickly die. Many other examples can of course be taken from medical practice, ranging from the dependency created by trauma, to the deliberately induced dependency of anaesthesia prior to surgery. In these examples there is really little to discuss: the dependency is necessary and inevitable and, in order to maintain the life and promote the health of the individual, dependency must be acknowledged and the needs met. In less dramatic form, all illness creates at least a period of necessary dependency. This is what Komrad has in mind,[16] and it is well described by Oliver Sacks in *A Leg to Stand On*:

> though as a sick patient, in hospital, one was reduced to moral infancy, this was not a malicious degradation, but a biological and spiritual need of the hurt creature. One had to go back, one had to regress, for one might indeed be as helpless as a child, whether one liked it, or willed it, or not. In hospital one became again a child with parents (parents who might be good or bad), and this might be felt as 'infantilising' and degrading, or as a sweet and sorely-needed nourishing.[17]

It is where the possibility of choice enters in or appears to enter in that we become less sure of the place of dependency in the moral scheme of things. Should we *create* dependency upon ourselves? Should we seek to be dependent on others? I would argue that neither autonomy nor dependency carry intrinsic moral value. It all depends on the circumstances. The autonomous crook is still a crook and the autonomous parent could well be guilty of neglect. In the examples which follow in the next section I wish to illustrate both the potential goodness and the potential harm which can stem from dependency, and to show its place in a realistic, unglamorous medical ethics.

TWO EXAMPLES

The dependent relative

The phenomenon of the dependent relative is not one which is discussed much in medical ethics – reflecting no doubt its hospital-biased and crisis-based origins. Yet here is an area where the community concern for the vulnerable is really put to the test. As the age profile of the population shifts to an ever-increasing elderly group, the phenomenon of dependency in *adult* life cannot be overlooked. Already in the 1990s more people are caring for adults than for children.[18] Despite a popular impression to the contrary only a tiny proportion of the over-65 age group is in institutional care (1.6 per cent are permanently in residential care; 2.1 per cent are permanently in hospital; a total of about 5 per cent are either in hospital or residential care, temporary or permanent, at any one time). Of course, a very large proportion of the remaining 95 per cent of the over-65s are not in need of special care, but it is clear that there are very significant numbers of people who do require care.

Who are the principal carers of this dependent elderly group? An Equal Opportunities Commission Survey (published in 1982) found that 42 per cent of carers were themselves over 60 (72 per cent over 50) and that the vast majority were women.[19] Moreover, the lower the socio-economic class, the more severe the dependency was likely to be and the less likely it was that the carer would have good access to support services.

What conclusions might we draw from this example? It illustrates that the phenomenon of permanent dependency is much more widespread than the 'blood and glory' style of medical ethics may choose to notice, and that this is likely to increase in the foreseeable future, thanks to the 'success' of life-saving or life-prolonging medicine. Of course dependency in this context is (or should be) only a part of the whole picture. An ethic which stresses respect for the wishes of the elderly, enhancement of their capabilities and the encouragement of independence is undoubtedly of central importance (and needs constant imaginative revitalization). But none of this can take away from the obvious vulnerability of the principal carers (relatives who are themselves advanced in years) which needs to be taken note of. Who cares for the carers? In a society where autonomy is regarded as supremely to be valued, those who seem to be coping are seen as moral exemplars – and left to get on with it. Furthermore, the inequality of the burden of care should be noted. Ill health is much more prevalent in the social class where the obligation to sacrifice oneself to care for a relative is likely to be more strongly felt and where the economic resources to enlist other help do not exist. The extremes of this inequality are the outcome of a political philosophy of *laissez-faire* liberalism, and are certainly totally out of harmony with a philosophy of respect for autonomy. But when autonomy *alone* is stressed, a much needed ethic of fair distribution based on compassion for the needy is often hard to find. In the real political world, as I have already observed, autonomy and self-reliance are often confused.

Mentally handicapped people

My second example entails a still more radical critique of the kind of society which stresses competence and self-sufficiency. It comes from the later sections of Hauerwas's *Suffering Presence*, in which he attacks current trends towards the elimination of mental handicap from society through selective abortion or new techniques in reproductive medicine. Hauerwas believes that the argument that thereby we are preventing suffering is a spurious one (for we imagine that to be mentally retarded is to be ourselves with normal faculties in that state of dependency). Instead, he argues, our real reason for wanting to eliminate retarded people is that we do not wish to face the moral challenge which they represent. Our basic state, he asserts, is not that portrayed by our cherished assumptions – independence, self-possession. It is really that of neediness and especially neediness for others to ensure our own survival and identity. Because we are loath to admit this we "naturally" disdain those who do not or cannot cover up their neediness. Prophetlike, the retarded only remind us of the insecurity hidden in our false sense of self-possession'.[20]

Hauerwas's argument is in danger of being a serious over simplification of the issues. Most obviously, he fails to make plain what degree of mental handicap he has in mind. He could be guilty of the idealization of some truly miserable states in reaction to an increasingly eugenic approach to the society of the future. But without undue sentimentalizing, there is still much to consider in the concept of the 'holy fool'. Do we genuinely respect and wish to learn from those whose autonomy is so severely restricted that they depend upon consistent daily stimulation to achieve any source of independence and choice? Obviously we will find the rational and self-regulating person easier to deal with than people of impaired intelligence and poor impulse control. Perhaps, too, we feel threatened by the total commitment and trustworthiness which such vulnerable beings demand of us. But the experience of relating to mentally handicapped people can remind us of the arrogance of our self-sufficiency; the need for focused and individualized concern emphasizes the essential blend of reason and emotion which genuine respect for autonomy entails. Perhaps the greatest damage Kant did to ethics was his logical, but pedantic and unhelpful, conclusion that since love cannot be commanded, it cannot be in any sense an emotion but must be merely an act of reason. Against this it must be asserted that the response of one human being to the need of another is a central component of the moral life.

A TENTATIVE CONCLUSION

It may be that this whole chapter is based on a misunderstanding or a misrepresentation. I observed at the outset that for a philosopher the obverse of autonomy is not dependency, but heteronomy – and these are clearly not the same thing. Moreover, respect of autonomy does not, in *theory*, lead to an arrogant, intellectualist, self-sufficiency but rather to an equitable treatment of all persons as worthy of respect. Again, as Komrad has observed, a philosophy based on respect for autonomy still sees a place for dependency (of a temporary kind) as a way of helping the individual back to greater self-regulation in the future.[21] But, at an empirical level, our attitudes to the vulnerable are easily affected by our own desires to be rational, free and independent and by our dislike of what we may see as a demeaning dependency which we would not wish for ourselves. To put the matter paradoxically, the stress on 'doing one's best for others' can certainly be paternalistic and patronizing – but so can our desire to foster autonomy if we fail to see the limitations of our own perception of it.

Thus I believe that there is a point in restoring to dependency (and the principle of beneficence which is its counterpart) a more central place in medical ethics. I am far from denying that respecting the autonomy of patients and seeking to enhance it when accident or illness have reduced its scope are highly important moral aims for the practice of medicine. But we must also accept that for some of us all of the time and for all of us some of the time the maintenance of autonomy will not be the major issue. Instead we need to know that we are responded to, loved, protected by people we can trust. We need an ethic for modern medicine which guides and sustains professionals and relatives when confronted by helplessness – their own and that of those they care for.

There is a moment in *King Lear* when kingship and folly meet: and Lear, in perceiving the (feigned) madness of Edgar and the loyalty of his own Fool, finally feels in his heart the vulnerable humanity they all share. My aim in this chapter has been to counterbalance our appropriate respect for *Homo sapiens* with the perception of our nakedness and incapacity so graphically described by Lear when confronted by Edgar:

> thou art the thing itself. Unaccommodated man is no more but such a poor, bare, forked animal as thou art.
>
> (Shakespeare, *King Lear*, III. 4)

NOTES

1 R. Gillon (1985) *Philosophical Medical Ethics*, London: Wiley, p. 60.
2 R. Lindley (1986) *Autonomy*, London: Macmillan.
3 J. Harris (1985) *The Value of Life*, London: Routledge & Kegan Paul.
4 ibid., p. 212.
5 See Lindley (1986), op. cit., ch. 5.
6 J. Benson (1983) 'Who is autonomous man?', *Philosophy* 58: 5–17.
7 ibid., p. 5.
8 ibid., p. 17.
9 A. V. Campbell (1984) *Moderated Love: A Theology of Professional Care*, London: SPCK.
10 ibid., p. 96.
11 For a full discussion of the relationship between paternalism and autonomy, see M. S. Komrad (1983) 'A defence of medical paternalism', *Journal of Medical Ethics* 9: 69–75.
12 S. Hauerwas (1986) *Suffering Presence*, Indiana: Notre Dame Press.
13 ibid., p. 7.
14 W. F. May (1983) *The Physician's Covenant: Images of the Healer in Medical Ethics*, Philadelphia, Pa: Westminster Press.
15 ibid., p. 115.
16 Komrad (1983), op. cit.
17 O. Sacks (1986) *A Leg to Stand On*, London: Pan, p. 128.

18 M. Marshall (undated) 'Some comments on the burden of care of dependent adults'.
19 Equal Opportunities Commission (1982) *Caring for the Elderly and Handicapped: Community Care Policies and Women's Lives*, London: EOC.
20 Hauerwas (1986), op. cit., p. 169.
21 Komrad (1983), op. cit.

8

SUICIDE AND JUSTIFIED PATERNALISM

Gavin Fairbairn[1]

The problems that arise when one is faced with attempted suicide or gestured suicide are both moral and practical in nature.[2] They are practical problems because they involve decisions about what one is going to do. They are moral problems because the reasons that one might have for acting in a particular way in relation to another person's self-harming will begin with one's beliefs about the value of human life, the value of autonomy and what it is to respect another as a person, and about whether paternalistic interference in another's life can be justified and if so, under what circumstances.

Suicide is devastating. It is an assault on our ideas of what living is about. In this chapter I want to discuss some of the moral problems that are raised by suicide and related human phenomena. They are problems that will be faced by those who occupy the middle ground between what I shall refer to as the 'liberal' and 'conservative' positions on suicide. It is difficult to predict who will fall into each of these two camps but religious beliefs apart, I think I am safe in predicting that the more contact a person has had or may have with suicide and self-harm, the more likely it is that she will be a suicide conservative.

By a 'liberal on suicide' I mean a person who believes that individuals are entitled to decide whether they live or die and that therefore anyone who attempts to kill himself because he wishes to die, should be allowed to die in peace. Someone who was committed to an extreme version of the liberal position would maintain that a person who has embarked upon a self-destructive course should be left to his fate by anyone who comes upon him, that we should not even attempt to determine whether his intention was to die. I do not believe there are many such liberals. A good test of whether extreme liberal pretensions were authentic would be to place a person who claimed to hold an extreme liberal view in front of a dearly loved friend who had cut his wrists or taken a massive overdose when she could see no earthly reason for him to wish to be dead.

A 'conservative on suicide' believes that whenever possible we should intervene in the self-destructive acts of others. There are as far as I can see two varieties of suicide conservative. The first consists of those who believe that suicide is simply wrong, perhaps against God's law and that anyone who is found trying to kill himself should be prevented from doing so because where possible what is sinful should be prevented. Such a person would be paternalistic to the extent that she believed it was in another's best interests to avoid doing what is wrong. The second variety is made up of those who believe that whatever God thinks (if there is God), to kill oneself is not something that a rational person could wish, that an individual who is acting suicidally must be psychologically disturbed, and hence that intervention to save his life would always be in his best interest. One could be doubly conservative by adhering to both of these positions.

I used to think of myself as a suicide liberal because I thought that suicide was simply a matter of personal choice, that a person had a right to do away with his life if he wished to do so. As a result I believed that someone who came across a suiciding individual should stand back and allow him to get on with it, that to interfere in another's suicide would be wrong. I thought this because I believe that taking personal responsibility for one's life is a very important feature of what is to function fully as a human person. Then, as a psychiatric social worker I had the experience of being asked to go out in the middle of the night to identify the body of a client who had just jumped in front of a car and of having another client pour a gallon of petrol over herself and set light to it, dying as the result of very extensive first degree burns. On numerous occasions distressed clients threatened to kill themselves unless I went to visit them immediately and on many others I had to offer help to clients who had attempted suicide unsuccessfully and to others who had gestured suicide successfully. On one occasion a client swallowed a large number of pills in my presence and on another I discovered a client lying in a pool of blood because following a large overdose which had damaged her stomach she had vomited up its contents. As a result of these and other experiences my attitudes changed.

SUICIDE, GESTURED SUICIDE AND COSMIC ROULETTE

Is suicide morally acceptable?

I think suicide should be thought of as self-killing rather than as self-murder because to think of it as self-murder pre-empts the question of whether it is morally right or wrong. All other things being equal, I think we are entitled to decide what to do with our lives. I think this even if our lives, both biological and biographical, are the gifts of God (and I am inclined towards this view). If life is the gift of God then He may reasonably expect us to treat it respectfully, to use it well and to give it up gracefully when the time is right. But I do not think He can expect us to hold on to it when it has no meaning for us any longer or it is unbearably painful to do so. Suicide may, but of course need not, amount to squandering the gift of life; but so may many ways of living the life which we have.

Although I think suicide is morally acceptable in itself, because our lives are our own and we can choose what to do with them, there will often be other important reasons why it is to be avoided. Those who enact suicide will very often leave behind them others, for example relations, friends or members of the caring professions, who will regret their demise.

A person who takes his life will most often be discovered by others when he is dead, thus involving them in his death in ways that may adversely affect them for ever. He may even, if his chosen method of suicide is sufficiently thoughtless, involve others in his dying, as is the case when a suicider jumps in front of a train or car, sets fire to himself in public or jumps from a building.

A person who attempts suicide in circumstances that involve others or mean that he may be discovered, offends against those who are inadvertently involved, or who discover him, because in acting as he does he fails to respect them as people who will be affected by his death. And this offence is not offensive in the same sense that it is offensive to pick one's nose or make love in public. It is an offence in the much stronger sense that it harms those who are offended against. Those who have had close personal contact with suicide are likely to understand what I mean here; I am referring, for example, to the psychological and at times physical distress that may be caused by, for example, recurrent visions of the sight which met one's eyes when one discovered a suicide or suicide gesture. A suiciding or suicide gesturing person may even intend to harm others by his actions. The extent to which a particular suicide is thus harmful, and the extent to which it was intended to harm, will suggest how morally acceptable it is.

So where suicide is morally wrong it is morally wrong because of the adverse effects it has on others; if no one is adversely affected I do not think that suicide is offensive or morally wrong.

Influences on our views of suicide

The ways in which we think about suicide are influenced by a number of factors including the religious and cultural context in which we have been raised. They are also influenced by the language we use.

We only have one word for self-harm that results or may result in death, no matter what its significance for the individual who dies or its effects on other people: 'suicide'. This poverty of language means that suicide, attempted and gestured suicide are frequently conflated with one another in a way that may result in moral and emotional confusion. Mary Rose Barrington draws attention to the importance language may assume in shaping attitudes:

> in itself the tendentious expression 'to commit suicide' is calculated to poison the unsuspecting mind with its false semantic overtones, for apart from the dangerous practice of committing oneself to an opinion, most other things committed are, as suicide once was, criminal offences.[3]

So the way in which we think about self-harming actions and about those who self-harm is influenced by the language we use to discuss such things. However, the dominant influence on our conception of suicide is probably the field of mental health.

Many, if not most, psychiatrists believe that suicide is almost always the result of maladaptive attitudes which need therapeutic help. Such psychiatrists share the conviction that the suicidal person is suffering from a rare disease or illness which is compelling him to try to kill himself and that medicine should intervene to treat the illness and prevent his self-destruction. However, though this is a commonly held view, there are dissenters from it even within the psychiatric community. For example, Thomas Szasz thinks that viewing suicide or attempted suicide as indicative of mental illness is 'erroneous because it treats an act as if it were a happening; and evil, because it serves to legitimize psychiatric force and fraud by justifying it as medical care and treatment'.[4] Szasz contends that the suicidal person is not *ipso facto* disturbed and that even if he is, this does not mean that he is mentally ill. He therefore refutes the claim that doctors should frustrate the desire of their patients to kill themselves because it is their duty to treat illness and that since the suicidal person is suicidal he must have an illness and therefore needs to be treated. I would not quarrel with Szasz's views about the myth of mental illness. However, the question of whether or not there is something called 'mental illness' from which a person who acts self-destructively must be suffering, and that justifies restraining him, is irrelevant to the question of whether at times a person who is acting self-destructively may justifiably be restrained. I shall discuss a range of circumstances in which it might be permissible to interfere in another's self-harming action later; none of these refers to mental illness.

The emphasis on the medical model of self-harm has led to the common belief that anyone who tries to kill himself must be 'depressed' in the sense of being mentally ill, rather than just miserably unhappy. This has, I think it is true to say, limited appreciation of the range of different acts that self-killing actions can represent and led to the whole range of self-harmings that can lead to death being subsumed under the umbrella concept 'suicide'.

To confuse acts of different kinds because superficially they look the same is mistaken and rather unhelpful. There is, for example, a great difference in the meanings to be attached to the acts performed by a psychiatric patient who ends up dead because he impulsively sets fire to his clothes, and one who calmly takes several days to gather together the materials necessary to burn himself to death.

Harré and Secord distinguish interestingly between 'acts', 'actions' and 'movements'.[5] Thinking about the distinction they make has helped me to come to a different understanding of human phenomena that are normally thought of in terms of suicide, in other words the things people sometimes do that might end in self-harm, even death. Perhaps the best way to explain is to offer an example. When I write my name, the *movements* I make may be described in purely physical terms. The *action* of signing my name is comprised of these movements but has some social or personal significance. Now depending on the context in which I sign my name the *act* I perform may be different. It may, for example, be the act of making a contract with someone, or signing a cheque or becoming married. So the same action may comprise different acts. The same act may be performed via different actions. The act of suicide, for example, may be performed via a wide range of actions including overdosing, cutting one's throat or wrists, putting one's head in a gas oven or leaping from a building. More importantly, notice that the same self-harming action – taking an overdose of pills, for example – may represent a number of different acts, from suicide to gestured suicide to cosmic roulette; I discuss the distinction between these and suicide in the next section.

Distinguishing suicide from other human phenomena

I take suicide to be the autonomous act of bringing about one's death by one's intentional action when that intentional action is intended to result in one's death. There are, of course, difficulties in telling when a person is acting, or has acted, autonomously – perhaps especially when he is already dead – and also in telling what his intention was. Though I believe it is possible for a person rationally to wish to die and to act in a way that is intended to bring about his death, I believe that what looks like suicide or attempted suicide as I have defined it, will often be something else because it will result from a less than autonomous decision.

Suicide is to be distinguished from bringing about one's death as a result of a range of similar human activities.

For example, it is to be distinguished from deaths that occur as a result of engaging in hazardous pursuits such as smoking, rock climbing and intravenous drug use. It is also to be distinguished from death resulting from intentional omissions where the intention was not to end up dead, as might be the case with an anorexic who persists in refusing food and dies as a result or a Jehovah's Witness who refuses a blood transfusion.[6] It is to be distinguished from acts where the person recognizes the possibility or even probability that he will end up dead but who intends not his own death but some other result; an example here would be where a person, heroically saving another's life, sacrifices his own. Suicide is also normally distinguished from deaths which, though intended and wished for by the dead person, result not from his actions but from those of others; I incline towards the view that voluntary euthanasia can often legitimately be considered as assisted suicide.[7] Suicide is to be distinguished from self-destructive actions in which people give up their fate to the cosmos and who, for example, take an overdose without calculating the amount needed to kill them, perhaps when they know that there is a good chance that someone will come by soon and discover what they have done. Such individuals do not calculate the odds of dying or surviving; they intend neither to die nor to live, but, perhaps acting on a whim, they indulge in a kind of cosmic roulette by taking actions that may or may not end in death. *Cosmic roulette* may result in lots of attention and help for the person should they end up alive; on the other hand it may result in death and an end to the troubles that precipitated the gamble. The cosmic gambler sees both as equally acceptable outcomes.[8]

Finally suicide is to be distinguished from *gestured suicide*. By gestured suicide I mean a self-destructive act that is not intended to end in death, but to fulfil some other purpose. For example, some gestured suicides are intended to punish others or to make them feel guilty or upset. Others are intended to draw attention to their agent and to his despair or need for help. Many people believe that suicidal behaviour most often represents a 'cry for help'. Though I have no doubt that some are indeed of this kind, I think that gestured suicide is more likely to be about controlling others than about asking them for help. It would be a mistake to view the actions of a suicide gesturer that went wrong and ended with him dead, as more significant than those of a suicider who through ignorance ended up alive.

Some people who take overdoses, cut their wrists, set fire to themselves and so on, have no intention of dying. In spite of this, if the circumstances suggest that a person has died as a result of an intentional self-harming action, there is a tendency to think in terms of suicide, although in general the verdict of the coroner will be suicide only where there is more direct evidence, such as a suicide note, that the individual intended to kill himself. The unwillingness of coroners to deliver suicide verdicts without strong evidence may mean that the true significance of some genuine suicides goes unnoticed. On the other hand, gestured suicides may be treated as if they are attempted or, when they are unsuccessful and end in death, as actual suicides. The problem, which is perhaps, but not necessarily, more difficult in the case of a person whose self-harming has ended up with him dead, is always in being sure of what an individual intended by such an action.

To treat those who survive gestured suicide as if they have attempted actual suicide will often be to give their actions more significance than they warrant. In making this point I am not suggesting that the gestured suicide is insignificant, only that most often it is less significant than intentionally taking one's life. Of course, it will often be difficult to distinguish gestured suicide from failed suicide and an individual who habitually attempts gestured suicide may eventually, or periodically even, attempt suicide.[9] Nevertheless it seems important for practical reasons to distinguish between gestured and actual or attempted suicide where possible, because to treat gestured suicide as if it is failed suicide may be harmful to the agent involved. For example, it may encourage him to engage in further behaviour of this kind as a way of gaining attention.

Where an individual who does not intend through a self-harming act to end up dead, but only to draw attention to his unhappiness, miscalculates, the fact of him lying dead in the end cannot change the nature of the act he performed; the consequence does not change the intentions or the act. And where an individual who intends to end up dead miscalculates and does not die, the fact of his being alive in the end cannot change the nature of the act he performed which was suicide, in this case unsuccessful. Of course the fact that he has not died might change his views – he might not wish to die any more – his brush with death may have changed his world view. But this does not change the nature of his suicide act.

Understanding suicide and other self-harming actions

There are a number of different dimensions in terms of which we would have to consider self-harmings in order to have any chance of understanding them fully. These relate to the intention of the individual – both in terms of his survival and in terms of the meaning he intends his act to have, to his rationality and finally to his success or otherwise in achieving what he set out to achieve if indeed he set out to achieve anything.

First, we would have to consider the individual's intention in physical terms – 'To be (dead) or not to be (dead)'. This will often be very difficult to assess. What, for example, should count as convincing evidence about what was actually intended by an individual who, for example, has taken an overdose which will prove fatal unless his stomach is cleaned out rather rapidly? Certainly it seems to me that a simple 'suicide note' will very often not be proof enough that he intended to die, unless there was other evidence that it had been written in a rational state. In other words in assessing the intentions of an individual who acts in suicidal ways, objective evidence may not give a foolproof means of deciding intention.

It is interesting to speculate whether a person could attempt to kill himself by performing some action that most people would be aware had no chance of bringing about his death. I think that he could because he might not realize what would be necessary in order to bring about his death. As a result such an individual might cut his wrists so that the blood trickled rather than gushed, or take a handful of vitamin pills because he entertained the false belief that this would kill him. Some people might question the seriousness of his intention because he had not made sure that his chosen method will actually bring about his death. However, the fact that his belief is a false one does not mean that his attempt at self-killing is inauthentic. People who do not have the knowledge or skill to pursue research into what does and what does not constitute a foolproof way of ensuring one's death, might nevertheless wish to be dead and to bring about their own death.

Second, we would have to consider the intention of the individual in a social and personal sense. What (apart from death or non-death) did he hope to achieve? Here we would want to explore the range of reasons a person might have for wishing to be dead or to take action that foreseeably will result in death even if death is not wished. I cannot enter here into a discussion of the various reasons that an individual might have for killing himself. However, there is, for example, a difference between the meanings to be attached to the deaths of a young man who kills himself because, having been paralysed in a car accident, he is desperately depressed at the idea of a life without sport, of a Buddhist monk who died in flames in protest during the war in Vietnam and of an old man who, missing his deceased wife, dies not so much because he wants to be dead but because he just does not want to live without her company. In each case though the act is that of deliberate self-killing, at another level the act is something different.

Third, we would have to consider the extent to which the agent's act was rational. In other words we would have to consider the extent to which he was aware of what he was doing. Was he aware, for example, that doing what he did might have the result that he would be dead afterwards and that death is not something one can relinquish having once achieved it?

Finally, we would have to consider the likelihood that the individual will be successful in achieving what he set out to achieve. For the intending suicider, success would mean death and failure would mean continued life. For the intending suicide gesturer, on the other hand, success would involve having whatever the desired effect was on other people. We might want to say that death, for him, would be a failure, though not a failure he would experience; alternatively, we might say that by losing his life the unsuccessful suicide gesturer has paid a greater price to achieve his purpose than he intended to pay.

PATERNALISM AND SUICIDE

I want now to turn to some of the moral questions that suicide raises. My main concern is with those it raises in relation to paternalism. Two questions suggest themselves.

1 First, when is it permissible to interfere in another's attempt to end his life?
2 Second, when is it permissible not to interfere in such an attempt?

These two questions approach the moral dilemma in which I am interested from both ends. The first represents the dilemma faced by someone who inclines towards the liberal view but is either worried about the possibility that some people may attempt suicide irrationally or, being aware that not all self-destructive acts are intended to end in death, worries about the possibility of allowing someone to die whose purpose was, for example, merely to draw attention to his unhappy situation. The second represents the dilemma faced by someone who, although inclined towards a secular version of the conservative view, nevertheless accepts that there may be times when an individual might have rational reasons for wishing to be dead when it might be a caring thing to do to allow him to die.

The reason that these questions present problems for those who are neither committed liberals nor conservatives on suicide is bound up with the problem of paternalism. For many people the idea of acting paternalistically towards others is distasteful if not all of the time, then most of the time.

In paternalism there is a conflict between what the person who is the object of the paternalistic behaviour wants and what others judge to be in his best interests. Paternalism is most often defined in terms of one person's acting in what she takes to be another person's best interests even when that other might wish to act otherwise. Richard Lindley suggests that paternalism has two legs.[10]

1 The agent is motivated by respect for the person who is the intended beneficiary of the act.
2 The will of this person (that is his or her current overall preference) is either disregarded or overridden by the agent.

Although I think that respecting another as a person will most often involve respecting his wishes there are circumstances in which I think one can override them without qualms. Suicide will often be such a situation.

A person who attempts suicide in such a way that others may discover him before he dies, cannot expect them to stand by and allow him to die. There are several reasons for this. For example, he cannot expect someone who does not share his views of the rightness and wrongness or rationality of suicide to act against her moral or rational beliefs in order to facilitate his demise by her omissions. In the event that his self-harming is discovered by a person with public responsibilities, such as a member of the caring professions or a police officer, a suicide attempter cannot expect to be allowed to die even when that other believes that he had good reason to wish to die, because to do so would put the career of the professional in jeopardy. And even if he is discovered by someone, free from public responsibilities, who believes that each person has a right to decide what to do with his life, a suicider cannot expect to be left undisturbed unless that other is convinced that to die is what he had in mind as the result of rational consideration and has extremely good reason to believe that the attempt will succeed.

I have argued that suiciders cannot expect to be allowed to die by those who find them. However, there are some exceptions. One of these would be where a suicidal individual has entered into an agreement with another to the effect that this other will not interfere. This might, for example, occur in circumstances where we may be inclined to think of a given 'suicide' as self-administered euthanasia; in such a situation an individual, who wished to be dead for good and rational reasons, would perhaps discuss his intention to end his life with close friends and relations and persuade them of the validity of his wish. It would seem wrong for anyone to go back on their word in relation to an agreement concerning a matter of such importance to the suicider. On the other hand it would be understandable if an individual who had made such an agreement developed cold feet when actually watching a loved one die by his own hand.

JUSTIFIED PATERNALISM

I have suggested that a person who wishes to kill himself cannot expect others to leave him if they discover him after he has taken suicidal action, but before he is dead, unless they have agreed beforehand that they will do this. I want now to discuss the case for paternalistic interference in the self-harming actions of others on four grounds. I shall then consider the case that may be made on the basis of what I shall refer to as self-interested pseudo-paternalism; this defence of the right to interfere in another's self-harming is, I think, the most powerful justification of all for such interference. A slightly less powerful defence may be put forward on the basis of one's concern for the interests of others.

I think it is reasonably clear that paternalism is justified in cases where we are aware that the suicider is not, or may not be, acting autonomously. For example, I think intervention may be justified for the following reasons:

1 Where the individual in question is badly informed.
2 Where the individual in question is lacking in rationality.
3 Where the individual in question is going to die unless we intervene but where it seems likely that his intention is something other than to bring about his death.
4 Where the person's autonomy interests are best served by intervention.

I shall discuss these reasons in turn.

Where the individual in question is badly informed

In the case of a person whose suicidal actions are based on false or incomplete information I think that we may be justified in intervening because we know something the suicider does not know which might affect his decision.

Lindley illustrates just such a justification for benevolent paternalism.[11] He relates the story of Theseus and the Minotaur. At the beginning of his voyage Theseus had said that on his return he would hoist a white sail if he had successfully slain the Minotaur; had he been killed his ship would return under its original black sail.

Unfortunately, though he did kill the Minotaur, Theseus forgot to change the sails and as a result sailed back home under a black sail. According to one version of the story his father Aegeus, assuming that Theseus was dead, leapt to his death from the Acropolis. Lindley argues that had we known of Theseus' success benevolent concern for Aegeus would at least have led us to try to inform him of this before he leapt. In terms of Aegeus' autonomy this seems unproblematic because autonomy involves acting in the way that we want to act. Aegeus wanted to jump only because he thought his son was dead, and if he had known that he was mistaken, he would have wanted rather to welcome him as a hero. So it would have been in the interests of Aegeus' autonomy that we should prevent him from killing himself. Lindley argues further, that if we could not persuade Aegeus of the facts we could justifiably have restrained him, either physically or by administering a narcotic, while still respecting him as a person. If this is the case, he argues, then not all paternalistic intervention is bad and in some cases it may even be required by benevolent concern.

Where the individual in question is lacking in rationality

On the grounds of rationality, paternalism may be justified in relation to two distinct groups. First, people who for reasons of immaturity (such as children), or intellectual impairment (for example people with severe learning difficulties or suffering from dementia), are unable to think through their actions properly in order to reach properly informed and responsible decisions. Difficulties arise here in determining the age or intellectual level at which we think a person is capable of the requisite degree of rational thought.

Another range of cases would be those in which we know that the person is psychologically disturbed at the time, for example by severe depression, such that though he thinks he knows what he is doing actually he does not. Of course it is difficult to say what constitutes a sufficient degree of disturbance. However, I take it as clear, for example, that we should not allow a person who is suffering from delusions to kill himself, at least in cases where his delusions are part of the rationale for attempting suicide. For example, I think it is clear that we should prevent a deluded person from setting fire to himself because he believed that this was the only way to kill the evil ants that were infesting his body and planning to take over the Earth.

Where the individual in question is going to die unless we intervene but where it seems likely that his intention is something other than to bring about his death

I think intervention in another's self-harming is justified where it is known, or for good reason believed, that the person does not intend to suicide but rather to gesture at suicide. This might be the case, for example, if a person habitually and dramatically took minor overdoses, or caused herself minor damage by cutting or scratching herself. This is not to say that such a person could not change from a habitual suicide gesturer into a suicider; indeed, as already pointed out, this seems to be quite a common occurrence. However, in such a case it would be as well to caution the person involved about the boy who cried 'wolf'. If such an individual wishes to kill himself he had clearly better do it in private.

Where the person's autonomy interests are best served by intervention

Beauchamp and Childress pose the question whether intervention in the name of saving a life is better than non-intervention in the name of autonomy.[12] They consider that people have a prima facie right to kill themselves which is entailed by the principle of autonomy, 'if persons act autonomously and do not seriously affect the interest of others, we ought not to intervene'.[13] As should be obvious from what I have already said, I have serious doubts about how possible it is for a person to kill himself without seriously affecting the interests of others. Things are in any case more complicated; in some instances intervention may actually take place in the name of autonomy as was the case with Aegeus in Lindley's discussion. Another example where intervention could be justified on the grounds that it would actually increase the suiciding individual's autonomy would be where an attempted suicide seems likely to fail with tragic results. In such a case if the attempt is not stopped the autonomy interests of the individual in question are likely to be injured. It could thus be argued that in order to protect his autonomy, interference in this agent's suicide attempt is required. Clearly this argument works only in circumstances in which we are aware that a suicide attempt is more likely to fail with horrible results than it is to be successful and things have not already gone so far as to have caused permanent damage. Things

126

would be different in the case of an individual whose self-harming behaviour seems very likely to result in death, because unless the attempt had already caused irreparable damage, as might be the case when an individual miscalculates in a gestured suicide involving a drug overdose, no adverse effects in terms of the individual's autonomy would ensue from our failure to stop the attempt. In the effects they have on an individual's autonomy, unsuccessful suicide attempts may be significantly different from successful ones. Whereas at least some failed suicides and unsuccessful gestured suicides will result in reduced autonomy, when suicide is successful it is not strictly true that the individual will have less autonomy in future. Being dead is not a state that people experience and hence a person who enacts suicide is not around to suffer any loss of autonomy.

Lindley discusses a case of this kind in arguing against exceptionless prohibitions. Though he thinks autonomy is important, he does not in general consider exceptionless prohibitions to be a good thing because they may 'subvert the substantive values which led to the prohibition in the first place'.[14] He discusses the case of John, who is desperately depressed and about to jump off a bridge. If it was the case, he argues, that we knew that John was most likely not to die, but to end up spending the rest of his life in a hospital bed, non-interference would result in our allowing his autonomy interests to be damaged. Were we bound by an exceptionless prohibition against paternalistic interference John's autonomy interests would thus be damaged more than they would by paternalistically intervening.

Even some writers who incline strongly towards the liberal view of suicide agree that on some occasions paternalistic intervention is permissible on the grounds that it is in the interests of the person's autonomy to do so. For example, though he believes it is wrong to interfere in suicide attempts which result from maximally autonomous decisions, John Harris believes that paternalistic interference is sometimes permissible.[15] He writes that it is in the interests of an individual to make a decision of such major importance as that whether to take his own life 'as autonomously as possible'. He believes that anyone who comes across a suicide may justifiably do their best to discover whether the decision is autonomous and to aid the person to make it as autonomous as possible:

> it is the act of someone with respect for others to try to stop the suicide for the purposes of ascertaining the cause of any distress that has prompted the action and attempting to remedy

it if possible. And of ensuring that the decision was maximally autonomous.[16]

Though it is easy enough to say this, in practice we are likely to have great difficulty in deciding whether a self-destructive act does result from a maximally autonomous decision. I find it difficult to decide how I would know a maximally autonomous decision if I came across one. How are we to decide that a person really wants to kill himself? Certainly finding a suicide note, or having heard a person say before taking an overdose that he wanted to die, will not be enough. Harris argues that though concern for the welfare of others is part of respect for persons, it must give ultimate priority to respect for their wishes. So he thinks that we can only intervene in suicides to remove doubt about whether the attempt is maximally autonomous. If the distress is irremediable or if the suicider doesn't want it remedied and his decision was maximally autonomous he thinks that a 'bystander must allow the agent to control his own destiny, if that is what he wants, and no longer obstruct the attempt'.[17] Harris's position here is founded on the idea that every person has the right to do what he wants with his life; he wants to protect this right both by refraining from interfering when he knows what the person wants and by interfering when he is unsure what the person wants. In doing this Harris fails to take account of the fact that those who find suiciders and suicide gesturers also have rights. I need not respect the wishes of others when to do so would cause me harm; and in this case they cannot expect me to respect their wishes.

There are some other problems with Harris's position. Apart from the fact that faced with a suicide or gestured suicide in the flesh rather than in the mind, it will typically be difficult to decide whether a person's decision was maximally autonomous, he fails to take account of the likelihood that those who come across suicides will not have the opportunity to ensure that the decision was maximally autonomous. For example, they will be unable to do this if the person they find has taken an overdose and is already unconscious. Nor will they be able to do it if, having stopped the attempt temporarily, the person is taken to a hospital for treatment. And, of course, a suiciding person may respond differently to the interventions of different people. For example, whereas an empathic and experienced counsellor might enable a person to make one decision, an insensitive and paternalistic interferer might push him in the opposite direction.[18]

THE SELF-DEFENCE JUSTIFICATION OF PATERNALISM

I want to end this chapter by saying something about the justification of interference in suicide on the basis that to do so amounts to self-defence. Strictly speaking what we are talking about here is not paternalism but what I would like to refer to as self-interested pseudo-paternalism which may be defined by modifying Lindley's definition of paternalism cited earlier, to read:

1 The agent may be construed as being motivated by (and/or may claim to motivated by) respect for the person who is the intended beneficiary of the act, but actually acts out of concern for herself or others.
2 The will of the person (that is his or her overall preference) is either disregarded or overridden by the agent.

In self-interested pseudo-paternalism the agent in questions acts out of concern not for the other but for herself. Notwithstanding what paternalistic interferers might say about their reasons for acting as they do, much of what passes for paternalism is really self-interested pseudo-paternalism because it is more concerned with protecting its perpetrator than with caring for the welfare of the individual in question. I do not intend to sound moralistic here; protecting one's own interests can in some circumstances be both understandable and morally acceptable. Indeed my argument is that self-interest is most often a sufficient justification for interfering in the suicidal actions of others.

Basically what I want to suggest is that when I come across a suicider I am justified in interfering if I do not want this person to die, and he had not negotiated with me that if I find him suiciding I will allow him to die.

I cannot avoid being involved in the outcome of a person's action if I find him suiciding, and since whether I act to save him or omit to do so, thus allowing him to die, I am implicated, I think that I can stop him because my feelings in this matter count, just as his do. Harris uses the expression 'bystanders' to refer to those who find suicides; this neutralizes their part in the event, but in practice many people who suicide are found either by relatives or friends or by people with public responsibilities: social workers, nurses, doctors, police officers and the like. Everyone who finds a suicider, dead or alive, has feelings, has moral beliefs, is vulnerable to the harm that involvement in a suicide can cause. To call those who find a person suiciding or suicide gesturing 'bystanders' denies that they have any real connection to the event. Earlier on I said a little about some of the experiences I have had of suicide; these are mirrored by those of many colleagues and friends with whom I have discussed the topic. I do not claim to have substantial empirical evidence of the harm that suicide can cause to those that Harris refers to as 'bystanders', though I think that it would be easy enough to obtain. However, I hazard a guess that most people who have had experiences similar to mine will have felt intimately and inextricably bound up emotionally and intellectually, with what was going on; hardly able just to view what was going on as if it were on television or as if it were a computer game. To adopt the view that intervention in self-harmings is wrong except where the person is acting non-autonomously is to fail to take account of the feelings of those who are involved. It does not seem right to me that those who stumble inadvertently upon suicide must suffer the consequences of allowing another to die if they do not wish to do so. In the case of professional carers I cannot see any reason why a person should jeopardize her career by allowing a person, for whom she is responsible, to die and being charged by others with neglect, or even, according to the doctrine of acts and omissions, with aiding his death, by allowing him to die.

So I think that interference in another person's suicide can be justified on the basis that if one does not one will be harmed: by the feelings one would have afterwards or by the effects on one's career. I think interference can also be justified on the basis that one is concerned to prevent harm to others: to the relatives and friends of the suiciding individual.

If a suicider does not want to be found, or rather, if he is concerned enough to make sure that he is not found, then he will take enough precautions in terms of time and method to ensure that he is not. I leave it to the imagination to work out how one might kill oneself without involving others; I shall note, however, that I think it is quite a difficult business, especially for those who meet with others on a daily basis and will hence be missed.

Although I think self-defence or the defence of others can justify paternalistic intervention to stop a person killing himself there are some cases that might count as exceptions and I should examine some of these briefly. One would be where the suffering that will come about as a result of the death is small, relative to the suffering the person will undergo if he survives the attempt. There are two possible types of case here.

The first case is where the person's anguish and pain is so great before the suiciding action that anything others might suffer as a result of his death would be small by comparison. An example would be where a person was suffering from some awful condition such as terminal cancer, and was in dreadful pain, where his family had suffered for a long time because of his illness, where no one would suffer materially as a result of his death and everyone believed that death would be a merciful release. A case of this kind seems closest in meaning to euthanasia in the sense that it involves the intention to bring about a peaceful death. It seems clear to me that we would be best not to interfere with this person's attempt should we find him. Of course, if we are uninvolved in his plans to die, we may be unaware of them and interfere because we care for him or believe that he is not acting autonomously. This just goes to show how important it is for a person to share his plans with others.

The second type of case where I think it could be best to let a suiciding person die, and perhaps even wrong to prevent him, is where because of the nature of the suicide attempt, the person's state after intervention would be so bad as to make any suffering that might have been caused to others had the attempt been allowed to succeed, small by comparison. This might be the case if the suicide attempt is well advanced; for example, where we discover a person who has taken a massive overdose and we are pretty sure that if we stop the attempt the person will be so badly damaged that his autonomy will be greatly reduced and/or his chances of having another go will be greatly diminished. So stopping a serious suicide attempt after it is well under way could mean that although we prevent the individual from dying, we do not prevent him from being badly damaged so that our good intentions result in a state of affairs just as horrible as that which we were trying to prevent; indeed some people might wish to argue that by stopping such an attempt we actually harmed the suiciding person. Anyone who comes across a serious self-harming situation is in a double bind because of the lack of certainty about the outcome of intervention, about whether, for example, it will save the person from a fate worse than death or rather condemn him to such a fate.

The difficulty in any situation in which one person finds another person suiciding is in making an accurate prediction about the likely after-effects of a given suicide attempt or suicide gesture or of intervention in it. In the case of the blood-vomiting client to whom I referred earlier, it was difficult to tell what her state might have been afterwards; indeed after being in a coma for eleven days she was told by the doctors that she was lucky not to have damaged her liver permanently. Perhaps if her liver had been dreadfully damaged, my stopping her suicide attempt could have been viewed as morally wrong because my suffering and the suffering of her family and friends had she died might have been less than hers had she survived in a dreadful state. But accurately predicting the future is beyond most of us and so perhaps had this been the outcome I would have been able to avoid moral condemnation on the grounds that I had acted to avoid harm that was more certain rather than harm that was less certain; surely that is not something for which a person may be ostracized.[19]

NOTES

1 I would like to express my thanks to the participants at the conference on *Autonomy and Consent* at the University of Manchester at which this paper was read in 1988, for their vigorous comments. Susan Fairbairn and Martin Stafford have made helpful comments and I am grateful to them for these.

2 I refer in this chapter to the impoverished language of self-harm and in writing it I have come to realize even more acutely the difficulties that this causes. For example, though I distinguish between suicide and various other self-harming activities such as gestured suicide and cosmic roulette, for the sake of brevity I often use the common language in my discussion. Thus, for example, at times I refer to 'suiciders' when it would be more accurate to say 'people who enact suicide or who gesture suicide or who otherwise act in ways that are self-harming that might conceivably end in their deaths'.

3 M. R. Barrington (1969) 'The case for rational suicide', in A. B. Downing and B. Smoker (eds) (1986) *Voluntary Euthanasia: Experts Debate the Right to Die*, London: Peter Owen.

4 T. Szasz (1971) 'The ethics of suicide', *Antioch Review* 31(1), reprinted in M. P. Battin and D. J. Mayo (eds) (1981) *Suicide: The Philosophical Issues*, London: Peter Owen.

5 R. Harré and P. Secord (1971) *The Explanation of Social Behaviour*, Oxford: Basil Blackwell.

6 Of course both of these could amount to suicide. Consider, for example, Angela, who was anorexic and gave up eating altogether because after

her boyfriend broke off their relationship, she could see no sense in living any longer. Consider also David, a deeply distressed Jehovah's Witness, who following a road accident refused blood more with the intention of ending his unhappiness than with the intention of obeying what he perceived to be a commandment of God.

7 In a similar way suicide may sometimes be thought of as self-administered euthanasia. Consider, for example, the man suffering with AIDS who told his friends that should things become very bad he would want euthanasia and informed them of his plan to take an overdose when he believed that the time was right for him to die.

8 Perhaps really there are two varieties of cosmic roulette. Calculated cosmic roulette would be where a person does something that might result in death knowing that there is a good, but not certain, chance that he will be discovered. Whimsical cosmic roulette would be where someone does something that may result in death without thinking about what the results might be.

9 Consider, for example, Donna, who had a long career as a self-harmer and suicide gesturer, whose gestures included overdosing, eating sharp objects, cutting herself and on one occasion setting fire to herself while she was an inpatient. Eventually she died after setting fire to herself in a public place.

10 R. Lindley (1988) 'Paternalism and caring', in G. J. Fairbairn and S. A. Fairbairn (eds) *Ethical Issues in Caring*, Aldershot: Gower.

11 ibid., p. 50.

12 T. L. Beauchamp and J. F. Childress (1983) *Principles of Biomedical Ethics* (2nd edn), New York and Oxford: Oxford University Press.

13 ibid., p. 99.

14 Lindley (1988), op. cit., p. 203.

15 J. Harris (1985) *The Value of Life*, London: Routledge & Kegan Paul.

16 ibid., p. 203.

17 ibid., p. 203.

18 The question of the direction in which a person might be persuaded is not simple. An empathic counsellor might have enabled one person to decide that he really and rationally did want to die but enabled another to see that really he wanted only to have an effect on others which he could achieve at a cost lower than his life. On the other hand, a paternalistic interferer might have used the force of her personality to persuade the first of these suiciders to refrain from killing himself while pushing the other so hard that he decided to do it just to show that he could.

19 As it happens I was, by chance, visiting Gloria just as she woke up. She turned to me and said 'Hello, I really meant it you know. I really meant to die.' I replied 'Yes. I know you meant it.' Then she said 'Do you know what though? I'm glad to be alive.'

9

INFORMED CONSENT AND THE GHOST OF BOLAM

Richard Lindley

In 1947, prior to having a minor operation, a patient was injected with the spinal anaesthetic nupercaine, by a specialist anaesthetist. The nupercaine was, in accordance with the common practice of the day, contained in glass ampoules which themselves were kept in a jar of phenol. The ampoules developed tiny cracks invisible to the naked eye, and some of the phenol percolated into the nupercaine. As a result the patient, one Roe, was permanently paralysed from the waist down. The risk of contamination of nupercaine by phenol was first recognized by the profession in 1951. Although Roe's case was heard by the Court of Appeal in 1954, he failed in an action for negligence against the anaesthetist's employer, the Ministry of Health.[1] Lord Denning pointed out that the duty of care owed by anaesthetists to their patients was determined by the state of professional knowledge and practice *at the time of the incident*. This is only reasonable, since knowledge and practice do change with time, and it would be unfair to hold medical practitioners liable for negligence when they are simply acting in accordance with the best medical opinions of the day.

In 1957 in the case of *Bolam* v. *Friern Hospital Management Committee*, a voluntary mental patient failed in an action for damages.[2] He had suffered from fractures of the pelvis following treatment by electroconvulsive therapy. In accordance with the then customary practice at the hospital he had not been given a muscle relaxant, which would have reduced the violence of muscle contractions which led to the fractures. Moreover, the restraining

134

devices used during the administration of the electricity were minimal, and the doctor had not informed the patient prior to the treatment of its attendant risks. At the trial expert witnesses were called for both sides – some arguing that the hospital's practice was in accordance with good medical practice, others arguing the reverse. How should such conflicts between experts be resolved by a court, when the issue is whether or not a doctor has been negligent in his treatment of a patient? What standard of care is required of a doctor for him to be able to resist the charge that he has acted negligently (without due care)? The following test for the standard of care owed by professionals (including doctors) to their patients was formulated in Bolam's case: the standard is 'the standard of the ordinary skilled person exercising and professing to have that special skill'. A doctor or surgeon is not to be held negligent if she acted in accordance with the practice accepted at that time as proper by a responsible body of medical opinion, notwithstanding that other doctors adopted different medical practices.

In Bolam's case, as in that of Roe, the issue concerned whether or not a doctor had been negligent in the *performance* of an operation. But it also concerned the issue of the duty to inform patients of the risks attendant upon treatment. A doctor has three main duties towards a patient: diagnosis, giving information and offering advice, and treatment. In this chapter I shall not address the question of the appropriate standard of care for diagnosis and treatment; for in these areas the *Bolam* test is relatively uncontroversial, and does not raise special problems concerning autonomy and informed consent.

In perhaps most cases of medical treatment the doctor and patient are in a position of 'informational inequality'. The doctor has specialist, often technical knowledge, about the patient's situation. The patient depends on the doctor for the information on the basis of which to choose one possible treatment or another. This situation gives doctors a special duty of care to their patients. In this chapter I shall be concerned with the standard of care which doctors owe their patients to inform them of the material facts about possible treatments which may be available to them. Nowhere is this problem more sharply focused than in the area of consent to surgery.

My title refers to the ghost of Bolam because in the 1985 House of Lords decision in *Sidaway* v. *Bethlem Royal Hospital Governors*, with a qualification to which I shall refer later, it was decided by a majority that the *Bolam* test should apply not only to diagnosis and treatment, but also to the giving of advice and information.[3]

CONSENT AND TRESPASS TO THE PERSON

It is a well-established principle of law and morality that individuals should have sovereignty over their own bodies. Simply to lay a hand on another, even without injuring her, in law can constitute a battery. For a surgeon to perform an operation on an unsuspecting patient who has not given consent is certainly a battery, and the patient would be able to claim damages whether or not she was injured, whether or not the doctor acted negligently and, most importantly, whether or not she would have consented had she been asked.[4]

But what constitutes consent? At one extreme we have cases where a patient (or his parent or guardian) does not give consent to any treatment at all. Here, if the treatment is given, the giver of the treatment is liable for the trespass to the person known as battery. Perhaps the most extreme example of this would be Gilbert Harman's fictitious case of the unsuspecting patient who is surreptitiously killed during the night so that his vital organs can be used to save the lives of six dying patients in need of transplants.[5]

Next there is the situation where a patient consents to treatment, but is given a treatment quite different from what he had consented to. The most likely cause of this is administrative error. Such a case was referred to by BRISTOW J. in the case of *Chatterton* v. *Gerson* (1981).[6] It was the case of a boy in Salford in the 1940s who was admitted to hospital for a tonsillectomy. Owing to an administrative error he was circumcised instead. Here, according to BRISTOW J., the appropriate action against the doctor would also be trespass to the person.

The underlying principle is that in order for 'consent' to be a defence to the charge of trespass to the person made against a doctor performing an operation the consent must be real. In other words the patient (or the patient's parent or guardian) must genuinely consent to the treatment in question.[7]

We now enter shark-infested waters. Suppose there is a patient who chronically suffers from moderately severe neck pains. She sees her consultant, a neurosurgeon, who advises her that there is a surgical procedure which could alleviate the pain. However, there is a slight risk of some nerve damage. She agrees to the operation which, owing to the intrinsic riskiness of the procedure, and without negligence on the part of the surgeon, causes damage to her spinal cord which leaves her permanently paralysed from the neck down.

This is roughly what happened in the 1983 case of *Hills* v. *Potter*.[8] In this case the plaintiff sued the surgeon for battery, alleging that although she had signed a consent form her consent was not genuine. It was not genuine, she alleged, because she had not been fully informed of the risks, which had been explained to her only in the most general terms, no mention having been made of the risk of paralysis. She failed in her action, and in this case the judge stated firmly: 'the framing of the action in battery is to be deplored'.

In England it is now established that in cases where an action is brought against a doctor for giving incomplete information to a patient, it has to be framed in negligence. This is highly significant, and marks a strong move on the parts of the courts to protect medical practitioners. It is significant because for an action in negligence to succeed the plaintiff actually has to prove that the negligent conduct caused the injury which is the basis of the claim, whereas an action in battery does not require proof of injury since it is actionable *per se*. This is crucial in the kind of case we are considering, since in a negligence action the plaintiff has to prove that she *would not have consented to* the procedure had she received the information which she alleges was not given to her. Where the risk of damage was small this burden of proof may be very difficult to discharge.

I shall not now address the question of whether the performance of an operation without having given the patient adequate information should be regarded as battery or merely negligence. In what follows I shall, following the decisions in *Chatterton* v. *Gerson*[9] and *Hills* v. *Potter*,[10] assume that the civil wrong done to patients in such cases is that of negligence – a breach of the duty of care which doctors owe their patients. The question is: 'What standard of care is appropriate for the giving of information to patients by doctors about possible treatment options?'

LORD BRIDGE'S JUDGMENT

In *Sidaway* v. *Bethlem*, where the House of Lords decided to apply the *Bolam* test to the standard of care required of doctors in informing patients of the risks and benefits of treatment options, a detailed judgment was given by Lord Bridge.[11] The main rival to the *Bolam* test is a doctrine of law common in North America, known as the doctrine of informed consent. Whereas in England the general rule is that it is for the medical profession to decide, in particular types of cases, how much information needs to be given to a patient for his consent to be 'real', in certain states of the United States, and in Canada, a doctrine of informed consent has emerged. There have been attempts to define an 'objective' test based on the informational needs of patients. In law an 'objective' test is not quite what it sounds like. It is usually a test of reasonableness, reasonableness to be decided by the court.

The rationale for the North American attempts to develop an objective test of *informed* consent is clear. The courts should take very seriously patients' rights to self-determination. The *Bolam* test leaves it entirely up to the medical profession to decide how much information they should have to give patients. Suppose (unlikely though this might be!) that a substantial body of doctors were *excessively* paternalistic. Patients who felt that they were entitled to more information would have no remedy. Furthermore, unlike the case of diagnosis and treatment, the question of degree of information which it is appropriate to give a patient is not obviously a technical medical matter. The doctor may be in the best position to determine what the likely risks and benefits of a particular kind of treatment will be; but she is not, in virtue of her position, necessarily in the best position to ascertain what is the choice her patient would make were she allowed to choose autonomously.

While the rationale for a doctrine of informed consent is clear there are serious practical difficulties in putting such a doctrine into effect. In the District of Columbia case of *Canterbury* v. *Spence* an attempt was made to lay down an objective criterion of what is a sufficient disclosure of risk for ensuring that the patient is enabled to make an intelligent choice.[12] Having rejected the idea that it should be for the medical profession to determine what was sufficient ROBINSON J. held:

> the issue on non-disclosure must be approached from the viewpoint of the reasonableness of the physician's divulgence in terms of what he knows or should know to be the patient's informational needs.

A risk is required to be disclosed

> when a reasonable person, in what the physician knows or should know to be the patient's position, would be likely to attach significance to the risk or cluster of risks in deciding whether or not to forego the proposed therapy.

This is conveniently referred to as 'the prudent patient' test. It gives the patient more protection than the *Bolam* test, and acknowledges the possibility that a responsible section of the medical profession, or even the entire profession, may be wrong in withholding from patients information about the risks of various treatment options. It specifically refers to patients' 'informational needs', and thus attaches direct weight to patients' rights to self-determination – to play an active role in deciding their own fate.

However, ROBINSON J.'s judgment was subjected to the severest criticism by Lord Bridge in the *Sidaway* case. He had three main objections. First, he claimed it ignored the realities of the doctor–patient relationship.

> The doctor cannot set out to educate the patient to his own standard of medical knowledge of all the relevant factors involved. He may take the view, certainly with some patients, that the very fact of his volunteering, without being asked, information of some remote risk involved in the treatment proposed, even though he describes it as remote, may lead to that risk assuming an undue significance in the patient's calculation.

His second objection was that it would be

> quite unrealistic in any medical negligence action to confine the expert medical evidence to an explanation of the primary medical factors involved and to deny the court the benefit of evidence of medical opinion and practice on the particular issue of disclosure.

Finally, he complained that the *Canterbury* proposals were

> so imprecise as to be almost meaningless. If it is to be left to individual judges to decide for themselves what 'a reasonable person in the patient's position' would consider a risk of sufficient significance that he should be told about it, the outcome of litigation in this field is likely to be quite unpredictable.

Lord Bridge therefore recommended that the *Bolam* test should determine the amount of information which a doctor has a duty to give a patient. He was, however, prepared to make one exception: where

> disclosure of a particular risk was so obviously necessary to an informed choice on the part of the patient that no reasonably

prudent medical man would fail to make it. The kind of case I have in mind would be an operation involving a substantial risk of grave adverse consequences, as for example [a] 10 per cent risk of a stroke from [an] operation.

BRIDGE CROSSED

While accepting that the prudent patient test may be difficult to apply, with respect, I find Lord Bridge's arguments unpersuasive against it and unconvincing. Of his three criticisms of the test proposed in *Canterbury* v. *Spence* the first and third are most significant. The second objection, about the need for expert witnesses, derives what force it has from the first objection (about the special nature of the doctor–patient relationship); and in any case, an 'objective' test would not be inconsistent with expert witness evidence being heard, although such evidence would have less weight than it currently commands.

Bridge's third objection – that the *prudent patient* test is too vague – need not be decisive against the kind of test proposed by the District of Columbia Court. Throughout the law of tort, especially in negligence cases, courts use the test of reasonableness which they have used at least since 1837.[13] If a 'reasonableness' test were introduced in the area of the standard of care required in the giving of information to patients about treatment options, there would inevitably be uncertainty in the early stages; but as case law developed standards of reasonableness would emerge, and the uncertainty would diminish.

This leaves the first objection, which is perhaps the most telling, and most interesting. It rests on the plausible claim that a doctor's skill includes not only diagnosis and treatment, but also an ability to communicate information to patients in a way which will simultaneously give the patient enough information to make an informed decision, and yet not have a harmful effect on the patient.

Communicating information to a patient about the risks of treatment, or of non-treatment, can produce one or both of two types of harm. First, it can lead to anxiety, fear, panic or depression. Second, because of the first effect, it may lead a patient irrationally to reject treatment.

Lord Bridge's first objection to the prudent patient test rests on the claim that the risks of such harms arising from a disclosure of information in a particular case will emerge only through the doctor–patient relationship, and therefore it would be wrong for the courts to decide what is appropriate irrespective of medical opinions.

The most obvious objection to this is that there is no reason to suppose that, for example, a neurosurgeon is especially well versed in the art of judging the psychological effects of particular disclosures on patients. It is true that they will, in time, have more experience of having given or withheld such information than will others. However, they may not be trained in psychotherapy, nor be in a position to observe longer-term psychological effects. Whether or not this is slightly unfair there is certainly a widely held public perception that surgeons are most at home with patients who are anaesthetized in theatre. There is certainly no reason why a brilliant neurosurgeon could not be inept at communicating with patients about the risks of treatment.

A second objection from the point of view of taking autonomy seriously is that the interests of the surgeon in being able to get on with the surgery may on occasion conflict with the patient's autonomy interests. It is quite true that a surgeon 'cannot set out to educate the patient to his own standard of medical knowledge of all the relevant factors involved'. This would be impossible through lack of time, and in some cases, through a patient's lack of educational capacity. However, it does not follow from this that *doctors* are necessarily best placed to determine policy about how much information should be revealed to a patient. Surgeons have an interest in there not being a duty to explain to their patients in great detail the nature of the risks of proposed procedures. In the *Sidaway* case the plaintiff was not complaining that she had not been educated up the standard of the doctor, but rather that she had not been told of the risk of paralysis down her left side. The risk, admittedly remote, was less than 1 per cent.

The most profound problem appears to be this: how much information about the risks and benefits of different options is it necessary to possess in order to make an autonomous choice? Put like this it does not seem to be a question which should be answered exclusively by surgeons or by their professional peers. Surgeons *are* in a privileged position when it comes to calculating the risks attendant upon various options. But they are not in a privileged position when it comes to deciding how much information is required for protecting the rights to self-determination of their patients. Nor, for that matter, are judges.

This is in part a psychological question, in part philosophical. I now turn to some of the philosophical issues.

AUTONOMY AND WELFARE

Let us suppose that a doctor's prime professional concern should be for her patients. This has at least two interpretations: for all those who happen to be her patients, or for all potential patients. The two are importantly different, since the first side-steps the question of selection and the distribution of the doctor's time between possible patients. Given that there are fewer doctor hours than can satisfy all patient needs it is inevitable that doctors will be unable to spend as much time on each patient as would be required for perfect treatment. Without a massive increase in the proportion of Gross National Product which is spent on medical care the only way of ensuring that each treated patient is given the best *possible* treatment is severely to restrict the number of patients treated. As this would be morally and (perhaps even now) politically unacceptable doctors and patients have to accept that the treatment they will receive is likely to be less than the best possible. Something has to be compromised. The question is 'what?' Although a doctor's prime professional responsibility is for her patients, it is impossible for a doctor to devote all her time and attention to any single patient. One of the key problems in the question of how much information doctors should be required to give to patients is that without extra staff more time spent on information-giving means less time spent performing operations, which means that fewer operations are performed and patients have to wait longer for operations, thus prolonging their pain and sometimes increasing the risks of deterioration and premature death.

Wherever there are fixed scarce resources there will be a tension between quality of care for each person treated and number of people treated. Our concern here is not with this problem as such, but rather to ascertain the minimum acceptable standard of care for patients who are being consulted by a doctor with a view to treatment. In order to ascertain what sort of (minimum) duty of care a doctor should owe a patient it is necessary to employ some theory of interests. The doctor is supposed to act in her patient's interests, but in the sort of case with which we are concerned it may not be clear where the patient's interests lie.

The doctor who gives a patient only general information about the risks of a treatment may claim to be acting in his patient's best interests for the sort of reason mentioned above by Lord Bridge – to spare the patient the pain of needless fear and anxiety, and to give the patient the best chance of actually receiving the treatment. On the other hand it might be pointed out that the patient has a *right* to know all the relevant facts about the proposed treatment. Is this a case where a patient's interests conflict with his rights? No.

People have interests that come from two sources – an interest in pleasure and the avoidance of pain which derives from our being sentient creatures, creatures capable of experience, and an interest in autonomy which derives from the fact that we are *rational* (as opposed to non-rational) creatures. Overpaternalistic doctors regard the interest in autonomy as *merely* derivative, in the sense that greater autonomy tends to increase pleasure. For them, where greater autonomy lessens someone's pleasure or increases her pain, other things being equal, autonomy should be sacrificed. On the other hand, some libertarians may claim that wherever there is a conflict between a person's autonomy interests and her mental-state interests (interests in pleasure and the avoidance of pain), the overall interests of the person require that the latter should always be sacrificed.

The view that in the situation described above there is a conflict between the patient's interests and her rights is confused. Rights derive ultimately from interests. What we have is a possible conflict between two types of interest. Where people believe a particular interest is very important and in danger of being overridden, the language of rights (moral rights) is frequently used. Here, it is said that the patient has a vital interest in autonomy, and that this interest should be respected, even if this would be against the patient's interests in the avoidance of pain.

On the view which I would wish to defend autonomy interests and mental-state interests are fundamental and irreducible to one another.[14] Each interest may be promoted or undermined to a greater or lesser extent; it is inevitable that sometimes trade-offs will have to be made between the two kinds of interest. Thus it may be in someone's interests to sacrifice a small degree of autonomy for a huge avoidance of pain, whereas it would not be if the loss of autonomy were greater, the avoidance of pain less. There is a serious problem of how the two interests should be calculated in particular cases, but this is a topic for another occasion.

The problem which I wish to address is what, in so far as a doctor has a duty to protect the autonomy interests of her patients, she ought to tell them about treatment options.

KNOWLEDGE, AUTONOMY AND DECISION-MAKING

Autonomy, literally 'self-rule', is best characterized negatively, by specifying types of heteronomy (its opposite). There are two basic types of heteronomy – cognitive and conative – although usually they occur together and may be hard to disentangle. Cognitive heteronomy has to do with beliefs.

An agent is cognitively heteronomous with respect to a particular belief or set of beliefs if either A holds that belief or set of beliefs on account of a failure of A's passive or active theoretical rationality, or the belief or set of beliefs is false.

Thus, one form of cognitive heteronomy is to be gullible – with insufficient reason to take the opinions of others on trust, lacking proper concern to establish their truth; another is simply to engage in faulty reasoning; perhaps the most common is what is sometimes called 'self-deception'; finally there is simply having false beliefs where there is no irrationality – either due to misinformation from another or through bad luck.

To be *conatively* heteronomous with respect to a particular action or set of actions, A must *act in a way which he judges, by his own values, to be worse than an available alternative*. An example of this would be someone who realized the need for cancer surgery but, perhaps through fear, refused to have the treatment.

It is clear from this that the interest in autonomy is complex, apart from there being two types of autonomy interest – interests in the development or maintenance of the capacity for autonomy and interests in its exercise. Furthermore, autonomy interests last through time, so that, for example, the current exercise of autonomy may be inconsistent with an individual's long-term, overall autonomy interests. Finally, it should be pointed out that nobody is perfectly autonomous, but that we are all more or less so.

Let us now attempt to apply this analysis to the problem of information being given by doctors about treatment options. Remember, at this part of the discussion we are assuming that a doctor, acting as agent of his patient, is seeking to protect or promote his patient's autonomy interests.

One duty of the doctor would be to try to ensure that the patient was not heteronomous in respect of his beliefs about the treatment options. This clearly imposes a duty not to lie – intentionally to inculcate a false belief. But the duty goes beyond that – particularly to try to ensure that the patient's beliefs are not based on inadequate grounds. For to have one's beliefs based on inadequate grounds is to be theoretically irrational, which is a form of cognitive heteronomy. This duty, in practice, is highly problematic.

As Lord Bridge pointed out, a doctor 'cannot set out to educate the patient to his own standard of medical knowledge of all the relevant factors'. On the other hand, within the realm of the possible there is a huge area of discretion. After the consultation the patient will believe either that a particular course of treatment (say surgery) is her best action, or that it is not, or she may remain uncertain. Let us suppose that after the consultation the patient believes that surgery is the best option. It is up to the doctor to have done what is possible to ensure that this belief is not founded on inadequate grounds.

If we were 'pure inquirers' in the sense Bernard Williams uses the expression in describing Descartes's method of doubt, we would never settle on beliefs until the evidence for them was decisive.[15] But we are not; we have other projects which are inconsistent with the project of pure inquiry. Given this, we shall never be completely autonomous with respect to our beliefs. The doctor's duty to his patient concerns the patient's autonomy interests as a whole.

The problem the doctor faces is, in this respect, similar to that of the individual agent acting for himself. Whenever I act or decide to act it is on the basis of certain desires and beliefs. The beliefs may turn out to be false; it follows that every decision I make is a gamble. How much time and energy should I expend on ensuring that the beliefs which motivate me are true? This will depend on the uncertainty of the belief, the seriousness of the consequences of the belief being false and the time available for decision. If I am contemplating crossing the Atlantic in a 25-foot yacht I would take more time to ascertain its seaworthiness than I would need to take before accepting that the QE2 is sufficiently seaworthy to risk sailing in her. Similarly I would not need to expend much time or energy before sailing my newly constructed model yacht on the village pond. If it did sink, this would be no disaster.

In the case of the doctor and the patient the doctor *has* the relevant information – more relevant information than she could practicably share. The doctor has to decide how much of it to reveal to the patient. It might seem that this should simply depend on the benefits to the patient (in terms of the patient's own projects) of the treatment, if things go badly, and on the doctor's estimate of the probabilities of success or failure, and the time available for consultation. Thus to take an extreme case: suppose a patient is suffering from acute appendicitis and will shortly die in agony unless given an appendectomy. It would be unreasonable to claim that the doctor should, in explaining the situation to her patient, have to describe in detail the possibility of the patient suffering from soreness or infection as a result of the operation.

An individual acting for himself always has to gamble about when he has done enough considering of relevant information before making a decision. The doctor acting for the patient must, in a sense, do the same. To make the *correct* decision in these circumstances may be very difficult.

But the doctor's situation is even more complicated. There is an important disanalogy between the situation of an agent deciding what to do for himself, and that of a doctor or other person trying to act in a benevolent role for someone else. Although it is true that autonomy interests exist through time, and hence are subject to temporal conflicts, an individual acting for himself *always* acts from his present perspective, that is in accordance with his present values and projects.[16] The doctor may and indeed often *has* to adopt a position which transcends the patient's current outlook. This poses a serious problem in the area of information-distribution.

A doctor should respect her patient's autonomy. In many cases this means to respect the patient's wishes. But what about a situation where a patient appears not to want to face up to the truth, or less dramatically, where a patient appears not to want to know about the detailed risks of a treatment? If the doctor insists on giving detailed information she is overriding the patient's supposed actual desires, and thus violating his conative autonomy. On the other hand, if she goes along with the patient's wishes and withholds information, she is also violating his autonomy, this time his cognitive autonomy.

Furthermore autonomy interests, like other interests, extend through time, and there are occasions where the only way to help a patient to become more autonomous in the future would be to *compel* her now to face unpalatable truths, painful though they may

146

be. In situations such as these a doctor cannot avoid infringing one or other of her patient's autonomy interests.

One interesting attempt to avoid this dilemma is to say that what is in a person's autonomy interests is what he would want were his wants based on true beliefs which took account of all relevant information. The proposed solution would be that the doctors should give the patient complete relevant information, even if the patient appears not to want this. However, this does not work because the acquisition of knowledge may in fact dramatically change a person's want-based interests. To take the most extreme case: given that I am not omniscient, it is not true that my actual interests are to have what I would want were I omniscient.

Suppose a patient has been diagnosed as having a form of cancer which will almost inevitably kill her within five years, although with medication, it is likely that the disease can be contained for three or four years without seriously affecting the patient's daily life. There is a slight chance of recovery, but it is *very* slight. Prima facie, respect for the patient's autonomy gives the doctor a reason for telling the patient that death within five years is almost inevitable. But suppose the patient is a writer who is working on her magnum opus which will probably be finished within three years, and the doctor knows that completion of this work is the patient's major life project. Suppose further that the doctor knows or has good reason to believe, that if the patient comes to believe that there is almost no chance of living beyond three years she will sink into a depression which will make her lose her appetite for life, and in particular her desire to complete her life's work. Should the doctor *then* be candid about the slim chances of recovery, even if the patient has not specifically asked him to be candid? The respect for the patient's current cognitive autonomy conflicts directly with respect for the patient's desire to complete her work.

It is not plausible to suppose that the doctor obviously should tell her the whole truth on the grounds that the desire to finish her work should be ignored since it would disappear if she acquired the (true) belief that death within five years was almost inevitable. To do this, as opposed to telling the patient that she had cancer which was subject to a remission of an indeterminate time, would ride roughshod over the patient's autonomy interests in completing the project. Related to this, but a *separate* point, is that the increased *cognitive* autonomy which the extra knowledge would bring could diminish, over time, the patient's long-term *cognitive* autonomy (say through denial), and her long-term *conative* autonomy (she might become incapable, because of her depression, of doing what she judges to be best).

CONCLUSION

The main point of the above discussion is to show just how complicated it is to decide what a person's autonomy interests are. Given that it is so hard to decide there is clearly much scope for non-culpable mistake. A failure to give full (or even adequate) information may well not be motivated by a negligent disregard for a patient's autonomy. For these reasons there is a good prima facie case for supporting the view that doctors need the protection of the courts in litigation in this area. The *Bolam* test provides such protection.

On the other hand, it is clear from the above discussion that the question of how to respect a patient's autonomy is not exclusively a technical medical question. Lord Bridge said it would be wrong to exclude the hearing of evidence from medical expert witnesses on whether a particular practice in regard to disclosing information was in line with a responsible body of medical opinion. But this does not exclude hearing evidence from others, including perhaps philosophers, lawyers and members of the Medical Patients' Association.

In her paper 'Patient autonomy and consent to treatment: the role of the law?', Margaret Brazier argues for the establishment by the Department of Health of a Standing Commission on Medicine, Law and Ethics, which would, as one of its first tasks, investigate the problem of informed consent.[17] The Standing Commission would be able to provide a legal framework for resolution of this problem, which has hitherto not been satisfactorily resolved by the courts in their case by case approach.

I would strongly endorse Brazier's proposal. She recommends that the composition of the commission should 'reflect medical and legal expertise and doctors' and patients' interests'. Many of the issues the commission would face, for example the questions 'What is an autonomous choice?' and 'Why is autonomy important?' are essentially philosophical, as the above discussion illustrates. I would therefore suggest that philosophers as well as doctors, lawyers and patients' groups should be represented on the commission.

NOTES

1 *Roe* v. *Ministry of Health* [1954] 2 Q.B. 66; 2 All E.R. 131.
2 *Bolam* v. *Friern Hospital Management Committee* [1957] 1 W.L.R. 582; [1957] 2 All E.R. 118.
3 *Sidaway* v. *Board of Governors of the Bethlem Royal Hospital and the Maudsley Hospital* [1985] A.C. 871.
4 See *Devi* v. *West Midlands Area Health Authority* (1980) *Current Law* 7:44.
5 G. Harman (1977) *The Nature of Morality*, New York: Oxford University Press.
6 *Chatterton* v. *Gerson* [1981] 1 All E.R. 257.
7 See Margaret Brazier, Chapter 4 in this volume.
8 *Hills* v. *Potter* [1983] 3 All E.R. 716; [1984] 1 W.L.R. 641.
9 *Chatterton* v. *Gerson* [1981] 1 All E.R. 257.
10 *Hills* v. *Potter* [1983] 3 All E.R. 716; [1984] 1 W.L.R. 641.
11 *Sidaway* v. *Board of Governors of the Bethlem Royal Hospital and the Maudsley Hospital* [1985] A.C. 871.
12 *Canterbury* v. *Spence* (1972) 464 F 2d 772.
13 *Vaughan* v. *Menlove* (1837) 3 Bing NC 468; [1835–42] All E.R. Rep 156.
14 This view is developed in R. Lindley (1986) *Autonomy*, London: Macmillan.
15 See B. Williams (1978) *Descartes: The Project of Pure Enquiry*, Harmondsworth: Penguin.
16 See Bernard Williams's paper, 'Persons, character and morality', reprinted in B. Williams (1981) *Moral Luck*, Cambridge: Cambridge University Press.
17 M. Brazier (1987) 'Patient autonomy and consent to treatment: the role of the law?', *Legal Studies* 7:169.

10

THE PATIENT'S RIGHT TO INFORMATION

Harry Lesser

A major issue in current medical ethics is the extent to which doctors are obliged to inform a patient about such things as their diagnosis of the patient's condition, their prognosis of how it is likely to develop and the likely advantages and disadvantages of possible types of treatment. The issue may be discussed in terms of the desirability of informing the patient, or in terms of whether the patient has a right to be informed. This chapter will focus on the second question, on the assumption that if there is a right to information then the whole issue can be settled on that basis, without having to consider questions of desirability.

However, before adopting such an approach one must face two problems about rights in general. The first is whether it makes sense to talk about rights in a purely moral context, rights other than those guaranteed by particular legal systems. Here, we should note that any system of rules, whether or not it is legally enforceable, and indeed whether or not it is explicitly put into words, can generate expectations and entitlements which can properly be called rights. We should note also that expressions of the form '*A* has a right to *X*' are often used to mean, not that *A* in fact has such a right, that it is guaranteed to him by the law or a code of rules, but that he *ought* to have the right. Putting these two points together, we can see that the question whether patients have a right to information is a perfectly sensible and intelligible one: it is the question whether either the law, or a generally accepted code of medical ethics, written or unwritten, ought to regard patients as entitled to certain sorts of information, and therefore to impose an obligation on medical staff to provide it. Whether this is best done by the law, a formal ethical code or an informal understanding, is a further very important question, outside the scope of this chapter.

The second problem concerns the desirability of treating the issue as one of rights. The notion of a right is essentially formal and legalistic; and to approach ethical issues in this way has both advantages and disadvantages. The advantages are that it makes the expectations clear and explicit, so that both doctor and patient know what they are entitled to and what is required of them, and that it helps to protect patients from any abuse of power by the professionals. The disadvantages are that it makes for a more formal, and less human and humane, relationship between doctor and patient, to the potential detriment of good medicine; that it may unduly restrict the doctor's options; that it may cause patients to complain or even to sue unjustifiably as well as justifiably; and that this last consequence may lead to the practice of defensive medicine rather than doing what is best for the patient. How one should weigh up these considerations is unclear, and probably it should be done differently for different issues. But in the case of information, one may suggest, the need to make things clear, to spell out to patients what they are entitled to know, is particularly strong. Hence it seems appropriate to treat this issue as one of rights, to ask whether patients ought to have any 'right to be informed' and, if they do, how far it should extend.

The answer to this depends on one's general view of patients' rights and of the appropriate relationship between doctor and patient. There are in effect two models of this relationship in operation. In practice they are often combined, or doctors may operate both, depending on the patient; but it will be convenient to treat them separately, while always bearing in mind that reality is rather more complex than this schematic treatment might imply.

The older, more traditional, model sees the patient, if they are adult and *compos mentis*, as having initially one right, the right either to authorize the doctor to act on their behalf or to withhold their authorization: the authorization may have to be made explicitly in writing, as when consent to an operation is given, or it may be implicit, as when the patient asks for treatment. In either case, 'informal consent', on this view, need only imply that patients know that they have agreed to be treated, not that they necessarily know exactly what the treatment will be or why it has been chosen.

Once patients have exercised this right, and empowered the doctor to act on their behalf, they acquire a new right – the right to the best possible medical treatment. Similarly, doctors acquire the obligation to do their best for the patient, and the right not to be prevented from doing their best: it is a logical point about rights and duties that, typically, what one has a duty to do one therefore has a right to do. And all questions such as what the patient ought to be told are to be settled in the light of this: if, in the doctor's honest professional judgement, good medicine requires that a particular patient be informed of the diagnosis, or the reasons for the treatment, or the risks attending it, the patient should be informed; if on the other hand the doctor considers that it would be medically beneficial to lie to the patient, the doctor should be prepared to lie – and it is worth noting that, although the attitude of the law has now changed, the right of a doctor to lie to a patient has in the past been upheld by the courts (for example in *Hatcher* v. *Black*, in 1954).[1]

x The alternative model sees the patients as retaining throughout their relationship with the doctor a right to autonomy, to make decisions themselves and not have them made on their behalf. On this view, the doctor, having made a diagnosis, should explain to the patient the various options available (which may include various possible treatments and also, sometimes, the option of doing nothing
x at all and letting matters take their course), their likely benefits and risks and any other relevant information, thus enabling patients to decide if they wish to proceed with treatment and, if so, which option they choose. It is then the task of doctors to carry out the patient's wishes to the best of their ability, whether by treatment, prescription or referral of the patient elsewhere. It may often in fact be the case that what the patient chooses is to allow the doctor to do what the doctor considers best: but this ought still to be the free choice of patients, not something imposed on them.

The adoption of this model clearly involves a much more extensive right to information. If patients have a right to make all the appropriate decisions, they must also have a right to all the information necessary for decision-making: the limits are set, not by what it is medically advisable or beneficial for them to know, but by what they need to know in order to make an informed assessment before deciding what to do. They may waive this right, and prefer to remain in ignorance and let the doctor decide: but the right must be theirs, even if they choose not to exercise it.

Moreover, it is this model, with its emphasis on the patient's autonomy, that is gaining ground: consciously or unconsciously, a growing number, both of professionals and lay people, see it as the way things ought to be, though they might not necessarily describe it in the terms I have used. This proves nothing, though, about whether it is a model that ought to be adopted: to consider this, we must turn to the merits and demerits of the two models.

The obvious merit of the older model is that it gives the power of decision to the person with the most relevant knowledge; doctors are not of course infallible, but they are more likely to be right than someone ignorant of medicine. However, matters are in practice by no means so simple. In the first place, there is not always a medically best course of action, for two reasons. One is that medicine has at least three aims – to prolong life, to remove obstacles to a person's physical and mental functioning and to relieve suffering. Very often these three come together; one could say that whatever achieves all three aims, for example, curing a disease that is both painful, incapacitating and life-threatening most efficiently, must be medically the best thing to do. But this is not always so; if, for example, the choice is to relieve pain at the cost of leaving patients feeling 'woozy' and confused, or to help them to be mentally alert at the cost of appreciable physical pain, then there is no 'better' course of action, even medically, except in terms of the individual patient's preference, whichever it may be: it is honourable to choose alertness at the price of physical suffering, but in no way dishonourable to choose the reverse.

It might be thought that this problem relates only to the choosing of ends: for example, whether to try to 'cure' or to try to relieve suffering, if one cannot do both. But the choice of means is also not a straightforward matter; and this brings us to the second problem. Even where the aim is clear, and agreed on by doctor and patient – for example to cure a particular disease or malfunctioning – it may not be possible to produce a 'right' or 'correct' ordering of the possible lines of treatment. This is because types of treatment can differ in at least five ways: in the likelihood of success, the degree of success possible, the seriousness of the 'side-effects' (which also are not all of the same type), the seriousness of the harm if things go wrong and the degree of risk that things might go wrong. And so, sometimes – though not always – decisions have to be made as to whether the near-certainty of improving a person's condition is better than the chance of totally curing it but also of doing no good at all, or whether this chance justifies some slight risk of doing very serious harm, or a high risk of painful but not damaging side-effects; and many more combinations are obviously possible. Once again, doctors' expertise enables them to know the possible consequences of various alternatives and to have some idea of their likelihood; but there is still no right answer to the question which alternative is best, which risks are worth taking and which are not, except in terms of what the patient chooses.

Moreover, this still assumes that the decision is purely a medical one: but sometimes it is not. Even if one can say – as sometimes one can – that a particular treatment is clearly medically best, that it is almost certain to work, that no other treatment will work, that the danger and discomfort is absolutely minimal, there may still be valid non-medical reasons for rejecting it: it may, for example, be vitally important for someone to postpone going into hospital in order to attend to essential family or business matters, even if medically they should go in at once. And although this is not always the case, only the patient is in a position to say whether it is or not.

All these considerations, that non-medical factors may have to be considered, that choices between options that have different advantages and disadvantages may have to be made, and that it is not predictable in advance when this applies, constitute, I think, sufficient grounds for saying that the proper person to make the decision is the patient, provided that the patient is adequately informed by the doctor. There are other reasons that can be given, notably the argument that each person is the best judge of what affects them personally and the argument that everyone has the right to make autonomous decisions. These may well be correct, but would require detailed consideration. It may therefore be best to confine oneself to the points just made, as being in themselves sufficient to refute the argument from expertise and to establish the right of patients to make their own decisions and hence the right to sufficient information to make a proper and reasonable decision.

However, to establish that this is a right that patients should be given raises two further problems. The first is the question of which patients have this right; the answer is both simple and complex. The simple answer is 'those patients who can understand the information sufficiently to make a decision based on it'; the complex problem is to decide who they are!

All one can do here is to indicate four categories of people that it would seem have to be excluded. The first is children; the problem is to decide at what age people become able to understand properly what they are told by a professional and to make decisions based on this understanding. In an ideal world this would presumably vary from person to person; in practice, some arbitrary point, hopefully right in most cases, has to be chosen.

The second problem arises at the other end of life, with those who are prevented by senility from making informed decisions. Here there are two issues – to decide who is in this category, and to consider how far this particular difficulty can be overcome by people making decisions in advance about what they want to be done under various conditions. Again, I do not want to go into the merits and demerits of such possibilities as 'living wills', but only to note the problem. It is also worth noting that there are other situations in which this could be used; in particular, it has been suggested that some decisions about what is to be done if things go wrong during labour might be best taken by a woman before its onset.

Third, there are people who are temporarily unable to absorb information or to reach a decision. Here, sometimes this is so obvious as to be unarguable, when the only question is that of who should take the decision on their behalf, and whether it should be the next-of-kin or a professional: this would apply to patients who are unconscious, drunk, drugged or delirious. More difficult is the patient who is mentally ill or mentally disturbed: the question of when a person becomes unable to make an autonomous decision is not an easy one to settle.

There is a similar problem with the fourth class, those who are permanently unable to make informed decisions: again, it is not always easy to say who does and who does not come in this category. A further problem, particularly with 'mentally deficient' persons, is that some people are able to absorb some sorts of information but not others, of apparently equal complexity, so that it is not always a matter of whether a person can or cannot make informed decisions, but of which kinds of informed decision they can make.

From all this we may conclude that the right to information should be extended to all patients who are able to make use of it. This excludes a number of categories of patient, some easy to identify and some very difficult: but it includes most adult patients most of the time. Moreover, even when a patient does not have a right to information in the way that the 'normal' person does, there may still be ways of preserving some of their autonomy. There may be, for example, better and worse ways of making decisions on their behalf; they may be able to take some decisions, though not all; they may be able to take decisions in advance on their own behalf. All this requires a great deal more work, both theoretical and practical.

It should be noted that, if this line of argument is correct, lack of education and lack of mental quickness are not grounds for being denied the right to information. Rather, they impose an obligation on the professional to give the information in a form that the layperson can understand and assimilate. This is an area where things are at the moment not entirely satisfactory: people have become increasingly aware that doctors, in particular, are given little training in communication, and that, although many doctors are excellent communicators, there are too many poor ones – too many occasions, for example, where a nurse has to explain to the patient the meaning of what the doctor has just told them. In other words the right to be informed must be a right to be informed in a way that one can understand; it is for the professional to adapt to the layperson as far as possible – as, indeed, is being increasingly recognized.

Moreover, there is an obligation to convey information humanely as well as intelligibly. This is something that involves institutions as well as individuals, because it involves such things as giving people time to assimilate bad news, and not expecting them instantly to get up and go home: this applies however gently the news is given. It also involves being prepared to say things more than once and on more than one occasion: there is evidence that the information that a condition is fatal simply cannot be accepted psychologically the first time, and has to be repeated. Indeed, both issues, that of intelligibility and that of humanity, are institutional rather than personal: where there are problems, these are probably often due, not to personal inadequacies on the part of the professional, but to an institutional failure to recognize the importance of effective and humane communication with patients, both at the stage of training and in the provisions made for giving information.

However, it might be objected at this point that we have now become wildly unrealistic, in two ways. First, to impose an obligation on already overworked professionals to give to every patient or client a full, clear and sympathetic explanation of everything relevant to their case is, it might be said, simply to ignore the limitations of time and energy. Second, large numbers of people, not necessarily either ill educated or unintelligent (and these are by no means the same thing), are either unable to follow detailed technical explanations or do not in the least want them: they would much prefer the decision to be taken on their behalf.

The second problem can, I think, be met by acknowledging that there is no reason why patients cannot waive their right to full information, and choose, still autonomously, to abide by what the doctor decides for them. Moreover, it is probably desirable that the doctor should make the task of them both easier by pointing out that she or he is perfectly prepared to do this: it would be wrong to make the point in a coercive or manipulative way, or to give the impression that the patient must leave the decision to the doctor; but to make it clear that this is one option seems very desirable. Indeed, there is some evidence that a sufficient number of people would choose this option to enable the first problem to be solved: in practice, the amount of information actually desired and required would not exceed what can be reasonably provided. What remains essential is that the choice be genuinely available and that full information will be provided if it is asked for.

But what constitutes full information in this context? It is worth remembering that literally to give full information would be in fact impossible: one could go on for ever describing the things that might happen if this or that treatment option were adopted. So a selection from what could be said has to be made, and judgement has to be exercised, on the basis of what it is most important to know in order to make an informed decision. Moreover, in decision-making, too much information can be as bad as too little: the amount given has to be restricted to what a layperson can cope with – and the experience of many lay people suggests that this is a strictly limited amount! This does not mean that lay people cannot make informed decisions, but that they need a relatively small amount of essential information rather than a mass of detail. The problem for the professional is to select this information in a way that genuinely sorts out what is most important rather than what will automatically produce the decision that they themselves believe is best.

There are two particular points of detail here. One is the problem of informing patients about the risks involved in various kinds of treatment, if there are any. On the one hand, if major risks are not mentioned, patients have every ground for complaint that they have not been properly informed. On the other hand, if too many dangers, all in themselves unlikely, are mentioned, this has the effect of presenting the patient with a distorted picture of the situation, of making the treatment seem more dangerous than it really is. The selection of information requires, it seems, not only sorting out what is important but also giving a balanced picture – one that gives fair weight to the advantages and the disadvantages of particular choices. As with the conditions of humanity and clarity, it is a matter not only of telling the truth but also of presenting it in a way that is helpful and useful.

There is a somewhat similar problem in telling patients about the physical pain and discomfort they may suffer. Since the expectation that something will hurt often makes it hurt more, it seems entirely legitimate that pain should be played down as a factor, even perhaps that doctors are quite right to speak in a code in which 'It won't hurt' actually means 'It won't hurt more than you can stand' – the hope being that this is not a lie but a self-fulfilling prophecy. But again, there are limits to this: patients utterly unprepared for the pain involved may justly feel aggrieved, particularly if a less painful treatment was available; they might feel this even if there was no reasonable alternative, on the ground that they wanted to prepare themselves for the ordeal. We are left once more with the problem of striking a suitable balance.

Similar considerations apply to the answering of patients' questions. The only difference is that the putting of the question, to which patients are entitled to an answer, may involve doctors in giving information of a kind that they had previously thought unnecessary. But given that it is now required, the same considerations operate – truth, humanity, clarity, selection of what is important, and balance. In particular, the patient has a right not to be lied to: this applies generally, but is most likely to happen in response to a direct question.

I have argued so far that all patients who are not incompetent in one of the ways outlined above should have the right to make their own decisions about such things as the line of treatment that they want (if there are alternatives), and that as a necessary condition of this they should have a right to all the necessary information, and a right to its being given clearly, humanely and in a way that aids decision-making. I have also argued that this can be done without deluging patients with unhelpful information, forcing them to take decisions they feel ill equipped or unwilling to take or making unreasonable demands on doctors and other professionals. In conclusion, I want now to consider four further problems, on the basis of these presumptions.

The first is whether considerations of humanity can justify overriding the right to be told the truth, or even the right not to be lied to, which is stronger: it is generally the case that there are many things one is not obliged to reveal but still ought not to lie about, although, given a right to information, this distinction may not often apply in these medical situations. It would seem that occasionally they can: if the doctor is really convinced that a patient cannot at the moment, or perhaps for the foreseeable future, handle a particular piece of distressing news, the right thing to do is surely to withhold the information or news and if necessary to lie. However, if what I have argued above is correct, the strong presumption should always be in favour of telling the truth: withholding information, and, even more so, lying, are for exceptional situations only. And there is evidence that in the past people have been much too ready to make these exceptions: it appears that the harm done by, for example, telling people that their condition is fatal has been greatly exaggerated, and the harm done by lying to them greatly underestimated. Nevertheless, common sense and humanity suggest that there are some situations in which the patient's right to information should be overridden; but they also suggest that this is rare, and much rarer than was previously thought.

The second problem is more specific, and concerns the giving of placebos. This is a 'treatment' that sometimes works well, and has the advantage of producing no side-effects; but it cannot work if the patient knows that the 'medicine' is a placebo. Perhaps this is a case for withholding information but not lying: the statement that the placebo will cure the patient is true, since it expresses a prediction the doctor honestly believes to be likely, and all the doctor has done is to refrain from saying why she or he thinks it will work!

Something similar can be said about the third case, that of the testing of a new treatment by means of a control group. Here, indeed, one can be entirely honest with the patients, by telling them that the treatment is being tested and that they will either be in the group given the new treatment or in the conventionally treated control group, but will not know which. It has sometimes been objected that, if one is as honest as this, no patient will be willing to take part in the test. But certainly some patients do – one group of AIDS patients in Australia, shown on British television in the late 1980s, is an example. Hence, though the situation requires withholding of information, it is a very 'above-board' withholding, in which patients know exactly what they are not being told, and why.

Finally, there is the question of whether patients should have access to their medical records. The issue here is a bit different: it is whether the argument given above applies, or whether some other justification is needed. It is true that a knowledge of what is on one's records is not normally relevant to the kind of decision-making with which we have been dealing. But it is relevant to the maintenance of one's autonomy in general, in various ways. One may, for example, feel – or even know – that something on the record is false and needs to be altered;

one may have forgotten the details of a previous treatment which are relevant to deciding what one now wishes to ask for; in general, seeing one's whole record may help one's decisions as a patient just as they help the medical staff. For these reasons, and no doubt for others, it would seem that one can justifiably include access of patients to their records as part of the conditions for making informed and autonomous decisions. And such decisions – including the decision to trust the choice made by the doctor – are desirable, if the argument of this chapter is correct, not merely because autonomy is in itself desirable, but also because they can make for better medicine and for more efficient treatment. It is not a matter of efficiency versus autonomy: efficiency actually requires the informed involvement of patients, and the combination of their knowledge of their own circumstances with the professional expertise of the doctor. The 'new' model of patients' rights should therefore be seen not as a constraint on the professionals but more positively, as working out more of the conditions for giving the best possible care.

NOTE

1 Discussed by Lord Denning (1979) *The Discipline of Law*, London: Butterworth, pp. 242–4.

11

STUDENT PROBLEMS AND PROBLEM STUDENTS

A vulnerable group?

Mary Lobjoit

Many of the problems to be discussed in this chapter are not uniquely those of students but, for reasons I shall try to explore, they do epitomize many of the dilemmas previously examined in this volume. I shall be focusing more on the issue of autonomy than on informed consent in this potentially vulnerable group. 'Psychotherapy matters because autonomy matters',[1] and as both a student health physician and a psychotherapist this is my starting-point when exploring the clinical issues arising in their practice.

Most of the ethical problems met with in the care of students,[2] whatever the form of their initial presentation, are related to how young people separate from their parents and family – establishing their autonomy. Particularly in the light of Alastair Campbell's account of the ongoing interrelationships between dependency and autonomy,[3] the casualties of the age group I am dealing with, I suggest, often represent the acute, intense state of oscillation and the rest of us the chronic striving to spend more time at the latter end of the spectrum.[4] It is the grey area between the extremes I want to examine: where ethical choices are often most difficult and there are no clear answers.

Many young people (even when they are technically domiciled at home) are itinerant, continually strive for independence, frequently change their lifestyles, are unwilling to use medical or related services unless absolutely necessary and are very conscious of the need for confidentiality – from school, college or university, employer or parental points of view. Support while young people come to terms with the realities of accepting responsibility for their actions is vital and one of the recurrent ethical dilemmas for the doctor is balancing the needs of the student-patient with the pressures of the family, educational institutions and society without stifling or prejudicing further development.[5] This is particularly so in the area of mental disturbance, where strenuous efforts have to be made to avoid premature diagnosis and labelling of what may be a transient form of behaviour. Because adolescents are extremely vulnerable while they are developing and experimenting, flexibility and tolerance need to be built in to the services provided for them.[6] Nicholas Malleson (of University College, London), who was one of those instrumental in the great improvements in student health care in the 1960s, wrote about this extensively and was deeply concerned about adolescent services in general, as well as those developing in institutes of higher education with which he was more familiar.

> How much has this problem been discussed! Adolescence is essentially a time of changing identities. In the whole business of growing up people do not just experiment with ideas about independence, or sex, or religion, they experiment with identities of themselves: they will be for a bit religious or irreligious people, they will be independent or they will be weak and lovelorn. To the outsider these sometimes rapid and radical swings go off and on so quickly as to seem like changing a suit of clothes, but to the adolescent himself they mean so much more – they are experimental changes of personality which feel very total at the time.[7]

THE PROBLEM STUDENTS

First I want to discuss the student, not as a member of a privileged group but as part of the whole adolescent community. Robert Hobson, a psychotherapist who has developed a method of therapy which has come to be known as the Conversational Model, distils his considerable experience within relationships in his writings and he says, in the chapter devoted to working towards a model of psychotherapy,

> Growing up is a repeated pattern of organisation, relative disorganisation and re-organisation. There is a recurrent loss of established states of order (characterised by differentiation and integration of experiences and actions) so that new forms of life may develop. There is a need for a balance of stability and change, with a continuity of significant personal relationships.

Unreal fears of painful loss, persisting from early childhood, can lead to inhibition of a process of growth and the realization of potentialities.[8]

This is not dissimilar from the consensus view, discussed in this series of contributions, of the process of struggling to attain autonomy. The adolescent is operating in that acutely vulnerable transitional area between dependence and autonomy – progressing, regressing and progressing again. This is the norm we accept but, as already stressed by Alastair Campbell,[9] and highlighted by Nicholas Malleson, we are all dependent at times (some permanently so) sooner as a result of trauma of some kind or later as a result of disease or ageing processes.

Second, students may become explicitly involved as psychotherapy patients. These have some further superimposed reason for their basic unhappiness, usually related to their family circumstances. Increasingly they, like many others, feel that such a therapeutic enterprise could be helpful in their quest for autonomy. In the conversation together we attempt to clarify the way he or she feels, so enhancing insight and the ability to attain and defend maximal autonomy in the face of continued difficulties. I quote from Hobson again, who focuses on the significant minutiae of the shared space between the therapist and the patient:

> Psychological problems arise when people use inappropriate ways of dealing with past hurts, especially those involving loss and separation. Means of avoiding pain (that is avoidance activities, customarily termed mechanisms of defence) can result in activities which hamper personal growth and the development of the dynamic relationship of aloneness-to-getherness. These defensive manoeuvres are usually associated with actual or feared conflicts.[10]

To reiterate – this personal problem-solving can be explored and tackled effectively only in the experience of being within a relationship. Mutual trust can diminish fear and avoidance reactions and by sharing a new language, with fresh ways of perceiving and acting in the world, problems can be explored and solved within the relationship.

In many ways students are ideal subjects for psychotherapy, bearing in mind their intrinsic vulnerability as previously outlined, but in general it can be said that they have not yet 'grown into' a (relatively) fully formed identity and they retain the capacity to develop and change. Their intelligence and curiosity, even when experiencing severe difficulties, are also important but may seduce the unwary therapist into exploitative situations. This imposes an even greater responsibility on the carer to act within a strict ethical framework but, as yet, no agreed code of practice exists for psychotherapy and much rests on the integrity of the individual to ensure the protection of the patient from incompetence and abuse. Jeremy Holmes (a psychiatrist/psychotherapist) and Richard Lindley (a philosopher, who has contributed Chapter 9 to this volume) look at the groundwork needed in order to establish such a code and in particular stress the need for the inclusion of something about deception because of the *fiduciary* (defined here briefly as contractual but described in more detail later) nature of the relationship:

> This is most clear in analytic psychotherapy where the professed aim of the therapy is to enable patients to become more autonomous by coming to understand and accept the truth about what they are really like, painful and difficult though this may be. This requires patients to place enormous trust in their therapists, and therefore makes them particularly vulnerable to manipulation and deception. Furthermore there is a special temptation for therapists, in order to save time, to employ strategies which rely on deception.[11]

Sidney Bloch and Terence Larkin also explore the ethics of psychotherapy and illustrate the need for constant vigilance with this example:

> the case of a student who had won a prestigious fellowship in order to write a book, but who had failed to write a word after nine months. It soon emerged that her motivation for doing the project was wholly derived from an unconscious wish to please her father, from whom she had always craved affection and recognition. Presenting him with academic achievement was her sole means of fulfilling this need. The therapist, an academically ambitious person himself, had to grapple with his own confused feeling, wanting his patient to succeed with the book – in accordance with a strongly held value that academic achievement was a worthy pursuit – and yet knowing through his clinical judgement that her 'ambitiousness' was ill-conceived and had caused her much misery throughout her life.

Thus a sort of 'value-testing' needs to occur constantly to ensure that the intrusion of values into the therapeutic relationship is never ignored but is dealt with in whatever way appears appropriate at the time. This approach will tend to preclude the unwitting imposition of values by the therapist onto the patient.[12]

The emphasis is thus directed towards enabling the student-patient to develop and nurture her autonomy while the therapist has the added responsibility of protecting both parties from foreseen and unforeseen dangers.

The third area I intend to consider is where the student is a *borderline* patient. This is a peculiar and ambiguous psychiatric category, difficult to define, and as a doctor, even more difficult to cope with.[13] These students represent one of the most vulnerable sections of the population, demanding both time and tolerance on the part of the carer. It is an American diagnostic term, used in a more restrictive way in Britain, to refer to the confusing area between personality disorder on the one hand and the neuroses and functional psychoses on the other. I shall elaborate later but the significant point for the discussion here is that patients typically have spells of normal function interspersed with transitory but intense excursions into impulsive self-destructive phases. They oscillate wildly across boundaries – their own and others. Their autonomy is fragile and their ability to sustain it is tenuous. In Britain a definable psychotic component is disputed but in the USA an aetiological link with borderline schizophrenia is acknowledged more readily. On both sides of the Atlantic it is accepted that such patients may at times also be depressed. These patients raise many ethical and medico-legal dilemmas in their management.[14] They frequently come into contact with the law both in the community and as it relates to the working of the Mental Health Act 1983.

THE STUDENT PROBLEMS

The word 'bizarre' (odd, fantastic, high spirited, extravagant – various dictionary definitions) tends to be used frequently in all three of these areas – the so-called normal adolescent, the patient in psychotherapy and certainly in the case of the borderline patient. It conveys the intuitive, gut feelings aroused when both the doctor and the patient are suspended in that area between the more definable positions of dependence and autonomy. We also have to take account of the notion that *time* is a factor which must be considered, first in the context of the sudden and rapid changes which can occur even in the most obviously *normal* members of this age group, with either sudden progressions towards maturity or temporary lapses into profound chaos and dependency. If I do make a judgement that a student's lack of understanding, his inability to sustain motivation and his subsequent failure to act all add up to the fact that his autonomy is impaired I have to make decisions about when and where to intervene. Second, how much time is available? Much of the most profitable learning comes from making mistakes but how long can one hold back before intervening, almost inevitably, in a paternalistic way? How long can a carer tolerate coping with the bizarre and regressive behaviour of borderline patients? And is it in their best interests if the self-destructive element of their way of dealing with life becomes dominant and it all ends in tragedy? I do believe, and it has been said elsewhere in this volume in other ways,[15] that my true concern and respect for the student-patient is not being exercised if I withdraw my intervention when it would actually be directed towards the ultimate restoration or improvement of autonomy. Is it not better to have a live, for the time being non-autonomous, person with the potential to restore her autonomy than an autonomous dead body as the result of a temporary blip on the road to maturity?

WHO IS NORMAL?

The main problem of course is that those patients we remember most vividly do not fit neatly into the three categories defined earlier. In addition, although the most telling of clinical vignettes are those which are true, I am using heavily disguised or hypothetical situations – some of which are quoted in the works of others. The only exception is my first case, who was someone who, at first sight anyway, belonged firmly to the group one accepts as containing normal adolescents. But I never knew her.

Joanna Palmer was a student at University of Manchester Institute of Science and Technology (UMIST) from 1968 to 1971 who later committed suicide. Much can be learnt about her in a paper given by Audrey Newsome in 1983 and retrospectively we have a lot to learn from her.[16] I suppose what I am saying about Joanna is that she was a tragic stage removed from many students. It could really only have been a very small step on the scale of normality, yet a very significant one in the context of her life. She did not seek help and presumably maximized her autonomy in engineering her own death. There was no chance to intervene. I find it very difficult to accept, and share in a degree of collective guilt to do with not being able to connect – again in Alastair Campbell's sense. But my conclusion here is that however hard we try to provide services dedicated to understanding the so-called normal adolescent, student or otherwise, we shall not always succeed in achieving a living, maximally autonomous person. Without evading responsibility or avoiding issues, we have to accept our failures too: we cannot be perfect and always manage to protect the vulnerable.[17]

The main causes of death in adolescence are accidents, suicide and malignancy. All are traumatic and each carries its own ethical burden. Risk-taking has to be accepted but dealing with the damaged survivors of accidents may produce lifelong problems. The survivors of suicide attempts challenge our respect for autonomy and the aggressive therapy used on young sufferers from malignant disease stimulates ethical debate about the quality of life acceptable to survivors. Addiction of many kinds is an increasing problem, not only to drugs but also to alcohol and tobacco. Eating disorders produce further instances where the doctor is a witness to the struggle for autonomy and a confirmation of the particular vulnerability of this age group.

My next case is that of a drug addict. Before coming to university he had been in prison for both using and selling heroin but had been fortunate enough to go through a successful rehabilitation programme after completion of his sentence. He found me soon after arriving in Manchester and I saw him regularly for three years; at no time did he disown the feeling that he would revert to taking heroin if he had any indication that he could succeed while using it regularly. He became dependent on me – I accepted the necessity and so did he. He graduated well and, as far as I know, has succeeded in maintaining his position. Maybe he has found someone else to absorb his dependent needs. We chose this way of dealing with the situation together and I hope that we managed to maximize his autonomy. But there is no escape from the conclusion that his modified dependency had definite survival value. Again there is an element of playing for time which is so vital in such a situation.

The more usual problems are not as extreme as suicide and drug addiction. At other times one may be lucky and be able to facilitate one of the rapid and less traumatic changes in position, even seeing a student daily over a short period or sharing the burden with other caring staff.

Sometimes the process of discovering autonomy may be painfully slow: a student in her final year had reached the end of the line as far as the university was concerned and she had not even realized that she could no longer pretend to continue her course. She had completely disengaged, was not in any obvious form of control over her life, appeared withdrawn and possibly was abusing drugs. Clearly she was unwell – thought, will and action seemed negligible, and yet she came voluntarily for help. To get her to take all the necessary steps herself – talking to people, writing appropriate letters – was a struggle but eventually she accomplished most of the tasks. We endured what seemed like hours of shared silence to achieve this but it was a joint enterprise, not a paternalistic one. She was on the way back to being able to act as an autonomous person.

I hope what all these cases illustrate is the complexity of the doctor–patient relationship in even the, at first sight, simplest group I delineated. In the other two scenarios the troubled student is brought into closer and more prolonged contact with the psychotherapeutic services.

A PSYCHOTHERAPEUTIC MODEL?

To illustrate the workings of the psychotherapeutic relationship I refer to work by Sidney Bloch and Allen Dyer.[18] They were dealing mainly with the issue of informed consent and the psychiatric patient but the latter part of the paper deals specifically with psychotherapy as a model for informed consent – 'a prototype for the relationship which is necessary for the optimal process of informed consent'. In general terms Bloch and Dyer agree that the dilemma between respect for a patient's autonomy and the need for some degree of paternalism is inescapable. Both autonomy and paternalism are dealt with in depth in the paper but they introduce the *fiduciary principle* as a third notion upon which the requirements of informed consent may be based. In this the doctor–patient relationship is defined as a relationship of trust, with at times appropriate and necessary phases of dependency, marking out the arena where the patient may trust the doctor sufficiently to disclose relevant material, knowing that the doctor will be competent and act on the patient's behalf and in planning how to proceed. This process occurs over time and develops from the beginning of treatment (psychotherapeutic or otherwise), unlike the legal situation, where the trustee decides *for* the client and then acts for him. Here the doctor decides *with* the client what to do; it is a form of partnership which is ongoing and Bloch and Dyer feel that caring and sensitivity are involved in the pursuit and maintenance of the highest ethical standards.

The principle of *partnership* represents the ethical ideal much more fundamentally than the paternalism of which the medical profession is often accused or the more impersonal injunction to have respect for autonomy, as an absolute, which is commonly substituted for it. They emphasize too the element of time available for decision-making and they set out two static formulations:

1 By acting paternalistically the doctor limits autonomy.
2 If the patient is autonomous she does not need to be dependent on the doctor.

These two states characterize situations which can arise at any time in a doctor–patient relationship but do not give any indication of their development over time or show how there is a constant oscillation between the two extremes. If the trusting alliance can be established; if both partners can work together to achieve the goal of understanding and clarifying the motives of the patient then there is a chance that these oscillations between dependency and paternalism will be used therapeutically. Dependence is recognized as intrinsic to the relationship and they observe that only in indifference does one treat a child or a dependent patient as completely autonomous.[19]

In the much discussed case of *Tarasoff* v. *The Regents of the University of California*, where a student was killed by her rejected suitor and compensation demanded by her parents for the fact that no warning was given by the therapist of her killer's expressed threats, it has been suggested that if this fiduciary type of relationship had been attempted the therapeutic arena would have been enlarged and the tragedy averted.[20] Actual decisions in the case were taken unilaterally: by the therapist, in his abortive attempt to break confidentiality and get the patient detained, and by the patient, who withdrew from therapy as a result of this. No one gained – least of all Tatiana Tarasoff. There was no therapeutic space, but as always it can be easy to find the answers in retrospect and one can only try to learn from such tragedies.

BORDERLINE PATIENTS

Having attempted to give a feeling of the kinds of problems encountered by students both in the wider setting and in the evolving relationship of a (psycho)therapeutic alliance my third section muddies the waters again. Borderline patients are very difficult and test the carer's autonomy almost to destruction. But that is the point – one cannot be destroyed because the aim of the treatment is to provide a long-term *holding* relationship with the aim of providing time; time in which there is the possibility of reduction of the *splitting* towards the therapist. To define briefly that means that the patient initially tends to relate to parts of other people, both good and bad, as they feel split themselves. This will obviously involve the therapist who becomes part of the system but together they work towards a feeling of wholeness within which the patient is enabled to feel comfortable in themselves and so can eventually separate from both the therapist and their parents. The essential clinical feature is a personality disorder in which there is instability in a variety of areas including interpersonal behaviour, mood and self-image. Interpersonal relationships are often tense and unstable with marked shifts of attitude over time. Frequently there is impulsive and unpredictable behaviour that is potentially physically self-damaging. Mood is often unstable with rapid shifts from normal mood to inappropriate intense anger. A profound identity disturbance may be manifested by uncertainty about self-image, gender identity or long-term goals and values. As I said earlier, for much of the time the person can seem to be normal and act in a completely normal manner. They rarely need hospitalization; in fact it is not advisable and medication is usually unhelpful. The aspect of their behaviour most relevant to these discussions is that of self-destruction. In working with students one inevitably finds a significant number who fit into this category and if there is sufficient tolerance within the system a favourable outcome usually ensues. Support for those engaging in this type of therapy is an absolute necessity in order to cope with both the problems of countertransference and the practical problems of dealing with those who continue to act out their difficulties.

Thomas Gutheil, an American psychiatrist, describes a number of cases of this type. He was mainly intent on exploring the medico-legal difficulties raised by these patients (more acute in the USA than they are here) but nevertheless the clinical management difficulties are vividly portrayed.[21] Part of Gutheil's thesis is that when lawyers are brought into situations where such patients are in conflict with their carers it is not always obvious that there is a real problem and that they may be unwittingly swept into accepting at face value the client's view of the situation. For the protection of the client it is essential that those legally involved with such patients are well briefed in the manifestations of the clinical syndrome. One of the most contentious areas is that of hospitalization. While it is generally the case that this is not wise, as indicated earlier, occasionally the chronic suicidal state which is very common in such patients is overridden by an acute situation where it is essential temporarily to detain the patient:

> Case 1: A hospitalized borderline patient convincingly mini-mized the seriousness of her recent overdose to her attorney, saying that her doctor was simply overreacting out of anxiety. The persuaded attorney pressed strenuously and successfully for her release. Once outside the hospital, the patient promptly overdosed again.[22]

The more usual variant is where a suicidal patient is denied hospital admission and the non-doctor may regard some of such clinical responses to those patients as uncaring, at first sight, but the risk of the patient killing herself by accident has to be weighed against the long-term advantage of modification of the behaviour:

> the evaluator's choice, largely by hindsight, seems to lie between two outcomes: a concrete dead body and the rather abstract notion of personal growth.[23]

These patients can be cured, or rather allowed to cure themselves, but it can take many years to achieve this. At the end of Gutheil's paper he quotes further case histories, emphasizing the importance for the treating clinician to see the main problem as the need to predict unreliability together with the patient, in an alliance-based co-operation:

> Case 7: A borderline patient attempted to disavow her responsi-bility for her future actions by stressing the unpredictability with which her impulses took control of her. The therapist's approach took this form: 'Let us accept together that you don't know at this time when suicidal feelings will strike. How can the two of us plan for you with that in mind?'
> By thus inviting the patient to share the risk of the situation

facing the dyad, the therapist brings the uncertainty into the realm of the therapeutic work, rather than feeling, oppositionally, that his task is to outguess the patient or foretell the future, feats outside the realm of the possible.[24]

The literature about these patients is vast and impossible to summarize either accurately or usefully here but the significant points are the resistance of the therapist to the temptation to take over responsibility for a patient's life and actively to seek their cooperation in all future planning whether it is based on certainties or not.

CONCLUSION

The idea of working together in an *alliance* is vitally important – it enhances the autonomy of the carer as well as that of the patient. It seems to work in widely differing contexts from potential long-term treatment, where a therapeutic alliance has to be laboriously forged, to more brief encounters between patient and carer where there is a need for informed consent to conventional medical treatment. I feel that it is an expression of what has long been implicit in the ethically acceptable practice of therapies, whether analytically or behaviourally based. But that is not to say that this way of thinking pertains at all times and therefore this reinforces the warnings we give ourselves about the vulnerability of these patients and the necessity to protect them from either the incompetent or those who misuse their power.

I hope that the case material quoted, both here and available in the references, underlines this importance of respecting the autonomy of students and complements the contributions of our other authors. Adolescence is a time of separation and for both students and their peers, who may be less privileged (particularly in an educational sense), these traumas tend to bring to the fore the issues discussed in this chapter. If the availability of resources for mental health care, and psychotherapeutic services in particular, ever becomes more universal as Holmes and Lindley cogently argue they should,[25] these qualifications about privilege could largely disappear. All would be able to shed their vulnerability and validate their own autonomy.

Issues of autonomy are universal and in all professional encounters the ultimate aim is to enable the client and the professional to participate on more equal terms. This idea is explored by a lawyer,

Harvey Teff, in his paper discussing consent to medical procedures.[26] There is a feeling that a sharing of responsibility could enhance the outcome in cases where the fiduciary principle, in its original legal sense, is applied in a less paternalistic way. So he also invokes the notion of the therapeutic alliance as a collaborative mechanism for increasing communication between doctors and their patients. This has the dual effect of encouraging mutual participation in treatment decisions together with the assessment of risks and outcomes; so facilitating the hope that litigation arising from such situations may be reduced. Thomas Gutheil also looks at these broader issues and tries to analyse why doctors and patients react defensively when treatment does not go according to plan.[27] As noted earlier in the psychiatric context,[28] he focuses on uncertainty as the primary threat to the doctor–patient alliance but in this paper he examines the whole area of clinical medicine. He sees informed consent as the focal point in establishing a therapeutic alliance and it becomes a powerful clinical tool which enhances honesty and acceptance of the realistic uncertainties in clinical practice.

The caring professions are learning much from these difficult situations but, as pointed out previously, we all bear the additional responsibility of protecting our clients, whether obviously vulnerable or potentially so, from exploitation. Enabling them to increase their autonomy is inevitably interwoven with all these activities.

NOTES

1 As argued forcefully in J. Holmes and R. Lindley (1989) *The Values of Psychotherapy*, Oxford: Oxford University Press, p. 142.
2 Personal communication to the working party which drew up the Pond Report: K. M. Boyd (ed.) (1987) *The Teaching of Medical Ethics*, London: IME Publications.
3 Alastair Campbell, Chapter 7 in this volume.
4 It is not intended to address the problems related more specifically to definable mental illnesses in this paper. But nevertheless many of the observations will also refer to those students, and their peers, who suffer in this way.
5 See note 2.
6 This becomes an even more difficult area because mental health services of all kinds are being affected by cuts and so reduced rather than expanded for this age group. Adolescent medicine as a whole has tended to be neglected but in my view the fact that students may be seen to have more privilege in this respect is not an argument to take services away from this group. It would make more sense if all members of this age group had access to better services and to mental health care in particular.

7 N. Malleson (1965) *A Handbook on British Student Health Services*, London: Pitman Medical, p. 57.
8 R. F. Hobson (1985) *Forms of Feeling: The Heart of Psychotherapy*, London: Tavistock, p. 183.
9 See Chapter 7 in this volume.
10 See Hobson (1985) op. cit., p. 183.
11 See Holmes and Lindley (1989) op. cit., pp. 188–203. Here they discuss the necessity for the development of a code of practice for psychotherapists which is interlinked with the establishment of psychotherapy as a profession, currently a controversial issue.
12 S. Bloch and T. Larkin (1989) 'Ethics in psychotherapy', in G. R. Dunstan and E. A. Shinebourne (eds) *Doctors' Decisions: Ethical Conflicts in Medical Practice*, Oxford: Oxford University Press, pp. 157–63 and in particular:

> We would contend that the therapist has a primary obligation to dispel the air of mystery through the process of informed consent. We would echo the claim of Redlich and Mollica [1976, 'Overview: ethical issues in contemporary psychiatry', *American Journal of Psychiatry* 133: 125–36] that 'informed consent is the basis of all psychiatric intervention and . . . without it no psychiatric intervention can be morally justified'. But we need to go further than this. The omnipresence of values in the practice of psychotherapy requires that informed consent be conceived as a dynamic process and therefore in need of repeated, detailed scrutiny throughout the course of treatment.

13 T. G. Gutheil (1985) 'Medicolegal pitfalls in the treatment of borderline patients', *American Journal of Psychiatry* 142 (1): 9–14.
14 ibid., p. 9.
15 See Alastair Campbell, Chapter 7, and Gavin Fairbairn, Chapter 8, in this volume.
16 Joanna Palmer made a bequest to UMIST to further the development of communication/counselling facilities there. She also wished funds to be made available to research students who were unable to obtain them from more orthodox sources. She wanted other students to have the help, both practical and therapeutic, which somehow eluded her. Audrey Newsome, formerly of the University of Keele and instrumental in fostering the theory and practice of counselling within student health services, was invited to give the inaugural lecture in the programme made possible by Joanna's bequest. The text of this lecture, and of subsequent ones, can be obtained from the Communications Office at University of Manchester Institute of Science and Technology, PO Box 88, Sackville Street, Manchester M60 1QD.
17 The necessity for supervision remains paramount both for the conduct of therapy and for the continued development of the therapist, as this is partly directed towards protecting the very real vulnerability of the latter.
18 A. R. Dyer and S. Bloch (1987) 'Informed consent and the psychiatric patient', *Journal of Medical Ethics* 13: 12–16.

19 ibid., p. 16.
20 L. R. Wulsin, H. J. Bursztajn and T. G. Gutheil (1983) 'Unexpected features of the Tarasoff decision: the therapeutic alliance and the "duty to warn"', *American Journal of Psychiatry* 140: 601–3.
21 See Gutheil (1985) op. cit., pp. 9–14.
22 ibid., p. 10.
23 ibid., p. 12.
24 ibid., p. 13.
25 See Holmes and Lindley (1989) op. cit. In chs 4 and 5 they give an account of the unjust distribution of psychotherapy and an exploration of its social role.
26 H. Teff (1985) 'Consent to medical procedures: paternalism, self-determination or therapeutic alliance', *Law Quarterly Review* 101: 432.
27 T. G. Gutheil, H. J. Bursztajn and A. Brodsky (1984) 'Malpractice prevention through the sharing of uncertainty: informed consent and the therapeutic alliance', *New England Journal of Medicine* 311: 49–51.
28 See note 13 for reference to Gutheil's psychiatric comments.

BIBLIOGRAPHY

In covering such a wide spectrum of both fact and opinion it is difficult to ensure that we have satisfied the readers' curiosity and needs for further references. So we include a selection of texts and more general works followed by a group of papers on more specialized aspects of the topics raised by our authors in the hope that beginners will find more detailed information and that others will find new areas to explore.

BOOKS: TEXTS AND GENERAL INTEREST

Appelbaum, P. S., Lidz, C. W. and Meisel, A. (eds) (1987) *Informed Consent: Legal Theory and Clinical Practice*, New York: Oxford University Press.

Barton, L. (ed.) (1988) *The Politics of Special Educational Needs*, London: Falmer Press.

Beauchamp, T. L. and Childress, J. F. (1979/1983/1989) *Principles of Biomedical Ethics*, New York and Oxford: Oxford University Press.

Bloch, S. and Chodoff, P. (eds) (1981) *Psychiatric Ethics*, Oxford: Oxford University Press.

Bok, S. (1978) *Lying: Moral Choice in Public and Private Life*, Hassocks: Harvester Press.

Bok, S. (1986) *Secrets: On the Ethics of Concealment and Revelation*, Oxford: Oxford University Press.

Brazier, M. (1987) *Medicine, Patients and the Law*, Harmondsworth: Pelican.

British Medical Association (1988) *Philosophy and Practice of Medical Ethics*, London: BMA, first published (1984) *The Handbook of Medical Ethics*.

British Medical Association (1988) *Rights and Responsibilities of Doctors*, London: BMA.

Buchanan, A. E. and Brock, D. W. (1989) *Deciding for Others: The Ethics of Surrogate Decision Making*, New York: Cambridge University Press.

Byrne, P. (ed.) (1987) *Medicine in Contemporary Society*, King's College Studies 1986–7, King Edward's Hospital Fund for London.

Cavadino, M. (1989) *Mental Health Law in Context: Doctor's Orders*, London: Dartmouth.

Committee on Abortion Rights and Against Sterilisation Abuse (CARASA) (1979) *Women Under Attack*, New York: CARASA.

Culver, C. M. and Gert, B. (1982) *Philosophy in Medicine*, Oxford: Oxford University Press.

Dunstan, G. R. and Seller, M. J. (eds) (1983) *Consent in Medicine: Convergence and Divergence in Tradition*, London: King Edward's Hospital Fund for London.

Dunstan, G. R. and Shinebourne, E. A. (eds) (1989) *Doctors' Decisions: Ethical Conflicts in Medical Practice*, Oxford: Oxford University Press.

Fairbairn, G. and Fairbairn, S. (eds) (1990) *Ethical Issues in Caring*, Aldershot: Gower.

Faulder, C. (1985) *Whose Body Is It? The Troubling Issue of Informed Consent*, London: Virago Press.

Freeman, M. D. A. (ed.) (1988) *Medicine, Ethics and the Law* (Current Legal Problems), London: Sweet & Maxwell.

Gillon, R. (1985/1986) *Philosophical Medical Ethics*, Chichester: John Wiley on behalf of the British Medical Journal.

Harris, J. (1985/1989) *The Value of Life: An Introduction to Medical Ethics*, London: Routledge & Kegan Paul.

Hicks, E. and Berg, J. (eds) (1988) *The Genetics of Mental Retardation: Biomedical, Psychosocial and Ethical Issues*, Dordrecht, Boston and London: Kluwer Academic Publishers.

Hirsch, S. R. and Harris, J. (1988) *Consent and the Incompetent Patient: Ethics, Law and Medicine*, London: Gaskell, Royal College of Psychiatrists.

Hobson, R. F. (1985) *Forms of Feeling: The Heart of Psychotherapy*, London: Tavistock.

Hoggett, B. M. (1990) *Mental Health Law* (3rd edn), London: Sweet & Maxwell.

Holmes, J. and Lindley, R. (1989) *The Values of Psychotherapy*, Oxford: Oxford University Press.

Johnson, A. G. (1990) *Pathways in Medical Ethics*, London: Edward Arnold.

Kennedy, I. M. (1988) *Treat Me Right: Essays in Medical Law and Ethics*, Oxford: Oxford University Press.

Kennedy, I. M. and Grubb, A. (1989) *Medical Law: Texts and Materials*, London: Butterworth.

Lakin, M. (1988) *Ethical Issues in the Psychotherapies*, New York: Oxford University Press.

Lamb, D. (1988) *Down the Slippery Slope*, London: Croom Helm.

Lindley, R. (1986) *Autonomy*, Basingstoke: Macmillan.

McLean, S. A. M. (1989) *A Patient's Right to Know: Information Disclosure – the Doctor and the Law*, London: Dartmouth.

McLean, S. A. M. and Maher, G. (eds) (1983) *Medicine, Morals and the Law*, Aldershot: Gower.

Mason, J. K. and McCall Smith, R. A. (1990) *Law and Medical Ethics* (3rd edn), London: Butterworth.

Petchesky, R. (1984) *Abortion and Women's Choice*, New York: Longman.

President's Commission for the Study of Ethical Problems in Medicine and Biomedical and Behavioural Research (1983) *Making Medical Decisions*, Washington, DC: US Government Printing Office.

Skegg, P. D. G. (1984) *Law, Ethics and Medicine: Studies in Medical Law*, Oxford: Clarendon Press.

Townsend, P. and Davidson, N. (eds) (1982) *Inequalities in Health (The Black Report)*, Harmondsworth: Pelican.

Veevers, J. E. (1980) *Childless by Choice*, Toronto: Butterworth.

Wulff, H. R., Pederson, S. A. and Rosenberg, R. (1986) *Philosophy of Medicine: An Introduction*, Oxford: Blackwell Scientific.

ARTICLES AND PAPERS

Bloch, S. and Dyer, A. R. (1987) 'Informed consent and the psychiatric patient', *Journal of Medical Ethics* 13(1): 12–16.

Bloch, S. and Larkin, T. (1989) 'Ethics in psychotherapy', in G. R. Dunstan and E. A. Shinebourne (eds) *Doctors' Decisions: Ethical Conflicts in Medical Practice*, Oxford: Oxford University Press.

Bradford-Hill, Sir A. (1963) 'Medical ethics in controlled trials', *British Medical Journal* April: 1,043–9.

Brazier, M. (1987) 'Patient autonomy and consent to medical treatment: the role of the law?', *Legal Studies* 7: 169.

Byrne, P. (1987) 'Review of the year 1. The ethics of medical research', in P. Byrne (ed.) *Medicine in Contemporary Society*, King's College Studies 1986–7, King Edward's Hospital Fund for London.

Dickens, B. M. (1981) 'The modern function and limits of parental rights', *Law Quarterly Review* 97: 462.

Englefinger, F. (1975) 'The unethical in medical ethics', *Annals of Internal Medicine* 83: 264–9.

Goldie, L. (1982) 'The ethics of telling the patient', *Journal of Medical Ethics* 8(3): 128–33.

Hoggett, B. (1986) 'Parents, children and medical treatment: the legal issues', in P. Byrne (ed.) *Rights and Wrongs in Medicine*, King's College Studies 1985–6, King Edward's Hospital Fund for London.

Karasu, T. (1981) 'Ethical aspects of psychotherapy', in S. Bloch and P. Chodoff (eds) *Psychiatric Ethics*, Oxford: Oxford University Press.

Kermani, E. J. and Drob, S. L. (1987) '*Tarasoff* decision: a decade later dilemma still faces psychotherapists', *American Journal of Psychotherapy* 41(2): 271–85.

Last, J. M. (1990) 'Guidelines on ethics for epidemiologists', *International Journal of Epidemiology* 19(1): 226–9.

Lord Scarman (1987) 'Law and medical practice', in P. Byrne (ed.) *Medicine and Contemporary Society*, King's College Studies 1986–7, King Edward's Hospital Fund for London.

Robertson, G. (1981) 'Informed consent to medical treatment', *Law Quarterly Review* 97: 102.

Teff, H. (1985) 'Consent to medical procedures: paternalism, self-determination or therapeutic alliance', *Law Quarterly Review* 101: 432.

Zigler, E., Hoddap, R. and Edison, M. (1990) 'From theory to practice in the care and education of the mentally retarded', *American Journal on Mental Retardation* 95: 1–39 (symposium).

INDEX

179